'This book is brilliant. It shines a [...] many women struggle to form qu[...] read for anyone who is afraid to s[...] women who need to be in contro[...]

author of *Guide to Superconfidence*, popular TV coach & founder of Consciouslyfemale.com

'Well done Annie. A contemporary and refreshing approach to revitalising your life and your relationships.' – Lynda Field, psychotherapist, coach and author of bestseller *Weekend Life Coach* and 16 other titles

'Annie's empowering, easy-to-read book shows exactly why she is one of the best, as it will teach and inspire you to become confident and take back control of your life and your relationships. If you seriously want to make changes, I highly recommend you read this book because if you apply these simple, yet powerful techniques, you will take your life to the next level.' – Gary Quinn, international bestselling author of *Living in the Spiritual Zone* and founder of Touchstone for Life Coaching, Los Angeles

'Annie's book is full of passion, humility and a wealth of experience. She both understands and expresses with flair and empathy the most important, enduring and significant relationship that any of us will ever have – the relationship with our own selves.' – Jo Hemmings, bestselling author and celebrity psychologist

'Annie Ashdown's authenticity and direct no-nonsense approach to delivering excellent standards of support for people wanting to move forward in their lives is what makes her one of Britain's Top Coaches. This book contains a wealth of wisdom, experience, insight and proven coaching tools and techniques that will enable you to gain the confidence to stop living your life based on the expectations of others and begin developing a life you love based on who you truly are. Well done Annie for leading the way and sharing your gift!' – Ian Banyard, Co Founder of Britain's Next Top Coach and Pathfinders TV

Doormat nor Diva be

How to win back control of your life and relationships

Annie Ashdown

First published in 2011 by
Infinite Ideas Limited
36 St Giles
Oxford
OX1 3LD
United Kingdom
www.infideas.com

A CIP catalogue record for this book is available from the British Library

ISBN 978–1–906821–91–3

Brand and product names are trademarks or registered trademarks of their respective owners.

Designed and typeset by Nicki Averill
Cover photograph by Claudine Hartzel – www.claudinehartzel.com
Printed and bound in Great Britain by CPI Group (UK) Ltd, Croydon, CR0 4YY

Though the contents of this book were checked at the time of going to press, the world wide web changes quickly. This means the publisher and author cannot guarantee the contents of any of the websites mentioned.

Contents

Acknowledgements

Si, you have shown me the power of a true union and unconditional love. You reflect my deepest feelings and highest values. With you I have found a duality, which is utterly magical. Thank you for entering my world.

Fiona Lindsay, you are without doubt the best agent in the business; *Doormat Nor Diva Be* would never have hit the shelves had it not been for you. Thank you for your constant belief and unwavering support. Your guidance, generosity, humour, integrity, humility, and professionalism blow me away. Limelight Celebrity Management: wow, I feel blessed to have such an amazing team like you guys guide me, support me and champion me. Alison, Mary and Mac, thank you for being such a remarkable team.

Jeremy Kyle, I so wanted you to write a few words for my book as you were utterly amazing to work with. You were professional, hysterically funny and incredibly supportive. I have never felt so at ease working with anybody as I did with you. You are a true professional and I feel humbled to have stood at your side. You have a huge heart and a wonderful spirit. I learnt a lot from you and I had the best ever time on the series. It was a real honour, pleasure and a privilege; I truly thank you.

I dedicate this book to my amazing father whom I miss so much every single day. Dad. You are always in my heart. Your words of wisdom have shaped me into the woman I am today. You taught me never to give up on my dreams, never to take no for an answer, to keep my values, be kind to others and true to myself. Thank you for instilling in me from an early age that other people's opinions were just that – opinions and not facts, and if they were negative not to let them throw me off track.

Mum, you insisted I was polite to everyone, respectful and considerate. Thank you; those disciplines have served me well. Your inner strength, persistence and single-mindedness always inspired me. You always said all you wished for me was that I find peace in my heart, and today I can honestly say that I finally have. Mum, I am sad you are not here to witness your wish come true. I miss you terribly.

Peter and David, you are the most amazing brothers I could wish for. You have constantly championed me and believed in me, always encouraging me to stand firm in my conviction against the face of adversity. You inspired me to be individualistic, independent and believe anything was possible. You have been great role models as you have walked your talk, and when you have fallen, you have got straight back up.

You have both been my springboards and I love you more than words can express.

Pat, Bob, Brian, Matthew, Andrew and Louise, I am really sad you are no longer in my life. I have never stopped loving you and I miss each one of you terribly.

Lesley Ashdown-Barr, Amanda Ashdown, Stephanie Ashdown, Danielle Ashdown, Alexandra Ashdown, I couldn't have wished for better sisters-in law and nieces. I feel truly blessed. You are all irreplaceable. I can totally be myself with you and even in the old days when I was a Diva you loved me unconditionally. You keep me grounded and real and most of all you always accept me as I am. I thank you for being my family. Your constant friendship, unconditional love and support means so much, and I don't know how I got so lucky to have you.

I feel so privileged to have such amazing clients over the past ten years. I feel truly humbled that so many trusted and continue to trust me with their deepest thoughts, beliefs and secrets. Thank you so much to those who have so generously shared their stories in this book.* I appreciate it hugely.

Thank you to my spiritual guides, healers and mentors who have relentlessly believed in me, inspired me, motivated me and lifted me up and carried me when my wings were broken. Noam Sagi, Michael

Hartzel, Teresa Symes, Kim Whitton, Skie Hummingbird, Christine Chung, Crystal Atlantis, Heather Loft, Moira, and Helen Johnson: I highly respect and value each one of you. Working with you has profoundly enhanced my life.

Nick Williams: thank you for being such a super coach.

Through all my 'ups' and 'downs' over the years I have been very blessed in that I have had a great tribe who have continually supported and championed 'Team Annie' and so I want to express a huge thank you from the bottom of my heart to: Adrian Bate, Dot Allison, Teresa Symes, Kim Whitton, Kim Carillo, Ruth Ospalla, Yasia Leiserach, Scott Buckland, Nikki Slade, Annabel Moorsom, Lisa Carlisle, Cath Counihan, Pavel Mikoloski, Sara Worsley, John Fallows, Gloria Salvucci, Steve Carrodus, Helen Storey, Stewie Scott, Bill Neeley, Debbie Harrison, Ian Banyard, Julia Brunton, Simon Rayner, Sara Woodhatch, Jayne Ball, Charlotte Heath Bullock, Michael James and Eiman Aslam.

And last, but by no means least, my great publishers Infinite Ideas. Thank you Rebecca Clare, Tim Moore, Kirsty Sinclair and Kate Santon, who edited this book. You are an ace, professional team and I have loved working with you and I want to thank you for taking such good care of my needs.

To the man who made my dreams come true – a big thank you from my heart, Richard Burton, for believing in my work.

*All names in case studies have been changed to protect the privacy of my clients.

Foreword – Jeremy Kyle

Annie and I worked together on twelve episodes of *Kyle's Academy* for ITV 1. Thinking back, the one word that springs to mind when I recall watching her at work is 'fantastic'. In fact, I think I told her at the time just how impressed I was with her methods and how she managed to really understand the problems we were faced with on that show and, more importantly, how to help to solve them. Anybody can call themselves a 'Life Coach' but it takes somebody like Annie to actually put the theory into practice and help people to help themselves in a practical way.

Introduction

Nothing is more empowering than standing up for ourselves

Over the last eleven years working as a coach and clinical hypnotherapist, I have come across so many clients and colleagues who strive to be perfect and cannot accept being anything less. They can't seem to grasp what I mean when I say that we need to strive for 'progress, not perfection'.

Life conditions us, tempts us, influences us, and we feed on the offerings it serves us. However, no one is perfect; the world isn't perfect. My English dictionary defines perfect as 'the state of being without a flaw or defect'.

So why should you take notice of what I say? Well, I have committed the last eleven years to helping others (especially women) to be true to themselves. After all, when we were born we had no fears, no negatives, no low self-esteem issues, no debts, no stress, no cynicism, and we were completely content with being 'perfectly imperfect' – so why can't we be like that today and accept who we are? So many women invest so much time in rehearsing to be someone they are not.

Doormat Nor Diva Be offers you:

- Clarity
- Support
- Encouragement
- Acceptance
- Awareness
- Tools for change

I am an intuitive coach, and not only do I offer proven techniques and pragmatic tools, but real-life experience. After all, why would you listen to me teaching you how to be self-confident if I told you I'd always been confident? Why would you trust me when I talk about why it is not a good look to be a Diva or a Doormat if I said I had never had these issues, if I said I'd always been a balanced person, someone who was never demanding or passive? Why would you listen to me on assertiveness if I revealed that I had always felt confident enough to ask for what I wanted?

I had an amazing father who taught me to never give up on my dreams and always keep my standards high and a mother who was shrouded in fear. She therefore suggested I take any job and any income and feel grateful to be employed, and settle for the first man who asked me out and be grateful for it, whereas Dad suggested that I set my visions high, not quit until I achieved them, not settle down too young and have fun until I met my ideal man and felt sure I wanted to settle down. As you can imagine, it was very confusing for me to hear two such conflicting views as a child. So how can I inspire you to make changes unless I had made them myself? How can I expect you to implement my suggestions if I haven't already implemented them myself?

For those of you who are not familiar with coaching or the sort of people who use coaches, let me explain that many athletes, entrepreneurs, bankers, captains of industry, celebrities, sales people, parents, lawyers, performers, authors – and 82% of companies – use coaches for one reason only: they work.

Awareness is a powerful catalyst for positive change and we need to become skilled at seeing what we need. This book takes self-care to a whole new level as I encourage you to engage in new daily habits by taking bold steps. Why would we expect anything less than the highest standards for ourselves?

This book will be like having a personal coach. I won't be mean on the motivation front as I know you have bought the book, so the chances are that you are already motivated enough to want to make changes. I passionately want to inspire you to do so. Just stop for a moment and imagine how it would be to speak to someone each week for an hour or more who is non-judgmental and who actively, genuinely listens to you; supports your visions, dreams and goals, who motivates you and is relentlessly devoted to you, encouraging you to take baby steps forward and helping you back up if you fall, while constantly telling you how amazing you are. Would that be incredible? Would you be able to fly? You bet you would. This is what coaching does for you. So why not ride this one by following my stream of suggestions, real-life experiences, strategies, tips and proven techniques, along with absorbing the catalogue of case studies? My only agenda is you, and moving you forward from where you are now in order to bring about tangible results.

It simply amazes me that we are in the twenty-first century and much has been written about boundaries, co-dependency, accepting and valuing ourselves, and yet so few of us do value ourselves, stand up for ourselves or ask for what we want and need at home or work. And the people who do so often tend to do it in a controlling, aggressive and demanding way.

I have seen endless clients and witnessed several friends and colleagues who allow partners, co-workers, family, friends and lovers to continually take advantage of them, and I have shockingly witnessed others who are the ones doing the mistreating. I hold regular workshops for women in London, and it is incredible how many are unaware of their own behaviour but attend hoping I can give them advice on how to change someone else: their partner, co-worker, family member or friend. I explain that my shining the light on their own part is not about shaming, judging or criticising them, but bringing awareness to them – which is the prerequisite for change – so they can rethink the actions, choices and decisions they are making and have a set of practical techniques and tools to use to attract and maintain healthy relationships. Many become elated, as they hadn't seen a way around changing their situation before. A few resist; clearly they are not ready to be accountable for their own behaviour and prefer to moan instead. I don't do moaning, so we part.

I do believe in healing wounds and past trauma through having therapy; however, I am not in favour of anyone spending years in therapy or becoming dependent on a therapist and searching for their approval. I find it far healthier for us to develop and trust our own intuition and start owning our power. Giving it away for so many years is what has led us to being a Doormat or Diva, someone with zero confidence and low self-esteem.

Two years into studying to become a psychotherapist I decided to quit and change direction. I trained as a coach, master practitioner clinical hypnotherapist, Louise Hay teacher, Theta energy healer and Emotional Freedom Technique practitioner so I could offer practical techniques to reframe limiting beliefs and raise people's confidence and self-esteem. I wanted to pass on the importance of heightened self-awareness and self-responsibility. What proof do I have that these methods work? Well, I can offer pages of testimonials from clients who had the courage to make changes. Most importantly, although I can't walk everyone's talk, I can certainly walk my own, and I do. I am a recovered Diva and Doormat, and applying these principles to my own issues resulted in my life changing profoundly. There is no stronger evidence than that.

Doormat Nor Diva Be is not a book on 'relationship addiction' or 'love addiction' or 'co-dependency' or 'how to bag your ideal partner' or 'how to fall in love'. There are plenty of those books on the market. Yes, I am aware that there are societal reasons, experimental beliefs, biological predispositions and childhood experiences all to be taken into account when looking at the way we behave. However, this book is not about untangling those issues. Neither is it an attempt to relive the wonderful experiences held in the 'Empowering Women' or 'Cocktails and Coaching' workshops I hold in London, where the support, incredible energy and humour is unique.

I learnt the hard way, and therefore felt compelled to write this book. Discovering the power we hold within ourselves can be a revelation. I don't have a degree in relationships or all the answers, but I do have years of experience of my own and have helped many clients build a healthy relationship first and foremost with themselves, and in turn this has brought about profound changes to their relationship with other people. Leaving behind Doormat and/or Diva behaviour transitions us into becoming empowered people. A well-respected producer in L.A had a meeting with me last year. He asked me 'What qualifies you to write on relationships?' and I replied, 'I have plenty of experience on how *not* to do them.' He then told me I had the perfect qualifications.

In my own self-exploration I realised I was allowing men to treat me in ways that were not honourable, respectable or acceptable. It was about Annie, not them. I never spoke out or said no. I allowed them to dump their Diva attitudes and behaviours all over me; I accepted their egos telling me what I should think, do and feel. It became clear, therefore, that I could not sit back and point the finger of blame at them as I had allowed them to remain in my life, even though their behaviour was toxic and selfish. When I saw I was being a Doormat and enabling them to walk all over me, I started to make huge changes within me, and started owning my power.

My journey has been challenging and, although I do not regret it, it definitely prompted my decision to write this book. At times it has been dark; at other times joyous. It has been harder rather than easier most days, and although my road was fraught with pain and darkness from an early age, somehow a little spark of light kept guiding me. I have been wise and I have been foolish. I have been loved by men and have loved with my heart and soul. Men have betrayed and abandoned me, but I hold my hand up and admit that I've hurt several men, although I have since made my amends. I have forgiven all of those whom I allowed to hurt and abuse me. Many times I have wanted to quit and felt utterly disillusioned, but somehow I found the strength to keep going with faith, hope and the belief that everyone enters my life for a reason, season or lifetime. At last I feel comfortable with being myself and rejoice in how liberating it feels to be authentic.

I swung from Doormat to Diva, and spent many years acting out as a Diva in relationships and believing the world revolved around me. In my role as a Doormat I realised that if I sat back and waited for these guys to see how controlling, cruel and unfair they were being to me I would be waiting for ever, so I needed to find my courage muscles and say my piece in a rational voice, one of reason and sanity. No one else's behaviour is our responsibility, we are only responsible for our own behaviour. It became clear that if my self-worth and inner confidence was solid, nobody could strip me down to my lowest point as I would not allow it to happen. We all deserve to be treated with love, respect and kindness, and if we attract people into our world who do not treat us in this way, it's down to us to stay or walk away.

So many women I coach, along with colleagues and friends, are either far too nice and therefore attract the wrong type of person, or are demanding bullies who attract submissive partners.

Doormats

Doormats don't know how to express themselves assertively, and often play games, use sarcasm, become resentful, sulk or manipulate others to get their own way. They don't always conform to the stereotype, being reserved and mousey; they can come in many disguises. Some mock other people but can't take it themselves, tend to avoid eye contact with others and smile when they feel angry, bottling up the anger within. I had a lot of suppressed anger as I was brought up to kneel in front of everyone, cap in hand, which resulted in severe on/off depression for twenty years as I turned my rage inwards.

Often Doormats moan and complain behind people's backs. They criticise, judge and are frequently conniving, and in fact many are passive-aggressive. Someone who is passive-aggressive won't tell other people face to face that they are angry with them and explain why; they will just smile and make out all is fine but behave in an underhand way by gossiping and making unkind remarks, or punishing their partners by withdrawing finance, love or sex. Some Doormats effectively castrate their partners by literally cutting them out of their life rather than being honest with them about wanting to split. Some are sweetness and light at work, and really sulky and intolerant with partners or with their children. It's pretty scary; Doormats can be so wrapped up in the delusion that pleasing themselves is selfish that they can be sucked into a relationship with a narcissist, or with someone passive-aggressive who appears to be charming but is an untreated addict, emotional bully or has violent tendencies.

Divas

Divas also don't know how to express themselves assertively and so are often aggressive, not realising the difference between a request and a demand. Many Divas believe they are assertive. They too bottle up feelings; however, when they do voice them, they often have glaring eyes and make unkind remarks, generally exploding when they don't get their own way. They tend to control and dominate people, and this leaves no room for healthy and honest communication. Their attitude is that their feelings and needs are far more important than anyone else's, and if getting their needs and wants met means treading on other people, that's fine. They are so wrapped up in themselves that others' opinions and views are of no importance. They are so deeply insecure that they need to be heard and have an insatiable desire to be right at all costs. Their blind spots are such that they often don't have a clue how egotistical or selfish they are by being so focused on pleasing themselves.

Both looks are so last season; I believe 2011 is craving authenticity. I am a big fan of Simon Cowell. He is completely honest: no pleasing others, no veneers, he states his truth. People always respect anyone who is honest as they would secretly like to be that brave themselves. We know where we stand with someone who tells it like it is, and Simon is not looking to win Golden Globes for people-pleasing. He says it as it is and it's been the making of him, and rightly so. He is one of the highest-paid men in television in both the UK and the US and is fast becoming a national treasure in both places.

Is he a Doormat? No way. Is he a Diva? No way. He is vigorously honest, fair, polite and generous, has integrity and – I know this from people who have had the pleasure of working with him – he treats everyone as an equal. He trusts his intuition and makes no apologies for being direct.

The objective of this book

This book's aim is to bring awareness to any woman who feels they are a Doormat or a Diva. I want to encourage every woman to be authentic and believe they are more than enough being who they are, and to embrace all their flaws and assets.

Get over trying to be perfect. It's a delusion; you will be constantly discontented if you spend your life trying to be someone you are not and striving for something which is an impossibility. Why waste your time? Acceptance is the key. Here's the paradox: the more approval we look for, the less we get. The less we look for, the more we get – like Simon Cowell. The thing is, whether you like him or not, he doesn't tap dance around people for affirmation. He states what he feels, which is authentic and vigorously honest.

I want you to step up your pace, really take a good long look at your behaviour. Call me your mind mentor, life strategist, inspirational coach, whatever you want; it doesn't interest me. What does interest me is you making a firm commitment to yourself to live a life where you stay true to yourself, your values, your beliefs and your dreams. This book is written to support you every step of the way. I want to demonstrate that you don't have to jump through emotional hoops to get your needs met. I will bring a wealth of examples, exercises and proof that we can all turn things around. I will provide a compass to navigate you out of the dark and into the light.

If you ever thought people would praise you and tell everyone what an angel you are because you let them walk all over you, you are so wrong; they will view you as the one they can take advantage of. And when you act in a demanding, aggressive way, they basically have even less respect for you, as they see you as being a bully. Being either a Doormat or a Diva is being a loser.

The bottom line is that Doormats and Divas don't have confidence or self-esteem, although many dispute this. If they had, they would stand upright in a relaxed manner, look people calmly in the eyes, ask for their needs and wants to be met in an honest, direct manner, and say what they mean and mean what they say. If they were in a dispute with somebody they would take the 'I love you, but I love me too' approach, and would be considerate to the other person as well as being considerate to themselves. Get the picture?

Let's get honest with each other here...

Let's be clear on this, many women have both Doormat and Diva traits. For example, I coach a lot of successful women who are empowered and courageous, yet when it comes to family, friends and men, they display Doormat traits.

My intention, therefore, throughout this book is to urge you to be yourself and get honest. I will illustrate simple things that many of you fabulous women do continually, perhaps without being aware of them – and if you are aware of them, then shame on you! This book offers raw and real stories, case studies and insights that will alter the way you think and behave. However, the tools and suggestions require total commitment and daily practice.

You will receive tips, resources tools and a game plan. My wish for you is that you get all the insights you need right now to support your changes.

The moving personal stories many clients have so generously agreed to share demonstrate how once we get acquainted with ourselves, learn to approve of our flaws as well as our abilities, we can turn our life around in a profound way. This book will inspire you with its vigorous energy and wisdom. It offers a different way of thinking which is realistic and straight to the point. Remember, ultimate success is not what you achieve but who you become aware of being in the process. Doubt and fear are partners; whatever you doubt will cause you to experience fear and whatever you fear creates doubt in your mind about your ability to deal with it. This book will take you from uncertainty to choosing your own path with courage and confidence. It will help you respond from a position of integrity and self-esteem rather than having knee-jerk reactions. You will be stimulated and challenged.

Get reading, get committed, get a notepad and start making changes so you can maximise your potential. Always remember, change comes from either inspiration or desperation. The choice is yours.

I will not be offering definitions or diagnostic criteria for co-dependence, depression or narcissism, as I prefer to allow psychological professionals to accomplish that task. What I do offer, from my own experience and the experiences of my clients, are real-life characteristic attitudes and behavioural patterns of both Doormats and Divas. After reading this book and implementing my simple yet effective and proven techniques, get ready for your confidence to rocket, your self-esteem to soar and your relationships to improve dramatically.

1 Am I a Doormat?

If someone is offensive to us, why wouldn't we tell them?

Many clients I coach bring me an issue around somebody or something in their life where they feel stuck and unsure how to make changes. I always ask them if they are willing to take a hundred per cent responsibility for their life to make the necessary changes, and they always say yes.

However, when it is a person-centred issue and I dig deeper, things can be different. I ask if they have discussed this issue or issues with the person concerned – for the purposes of this book, as we are focusing on relationships – and these are a few of the responses I hear time and time again:

- If I put my needs over theirs, that's being selfish.
- If I say what I mean, he/she may leave me.
- I don't like to say no, as I don't like to rock the boat.
- I've tried to say what's going on in my mind, but then I panic and end up saying nothing.
- I don't like to sound mean or upset anyone.
- I think maybe I am making a fuss; after all, they don't really mean it.
- I clam up or I ramble and digress from the issue.

How can we make changes and expect things to improve if, firstly, we are not prepared to face the reality of the situation, and secondly, we are not willing to walk through our fears? Why would we place what's going on in someone else's head above what's going on in our own?

Why do we feel we must kneel in front of others? For every reason why it isn't possible to say something, there are thousands of people who have been in the same situation and who, by saying something, have brought about profound changes in their lives.

It is not down to anyone else to mind read and guess what we want and need; it is not external conditions or circumstances that stop us. It is us stopping ourselves by not being prepared to walk through our fears.

I used to get so annoyed when I said to my partner that I wanted to talk, as although initially he often appeared happy to sit and listen, when I began to speak he would leap in and give me advice. Basically, he was walking all over my feelings and not respecting me at all. I wasn't asking him to solve my problem; I needed to express how I felt and then be given a hug. Advice is cheap, and all it did was make me feel even more inadequate and inferior. The thing that made me want to scream even more was someone jumping in and speaking over me before I had a chance to say my piece – but as a Doormat I never had the confidence to let him know how upset it made me.

We can think limiting thoughts, defend our self-destructive behaviours and ignore positive feedback. We can waste time moaning to friends, avoid necessary confrontation, not ask for what we want or need and keep repeating old habits, and then wonder why things are not changing – or we can use the exercises and techniques in this book to make changes. It's our choice. We have total control over our thoughts and behaviour. No amount of complaining is going to change the other person or the situation. Here's the thing: our relationship to love is a precise reflection of our most deeply held beliefs about ourselves.

Here are a few brief case studies some clients have kindly agreed to share from one of my assertiveness workshops. Names have been changed to protect their privacy.

Mandy is a 37-year-old nurse and lives in London:

'I'm a nurse and work in a busy casualty department at a London hospital. My hours are long, so I do tend to get ratty as work is so stressful. I rarely finish on time, and I am not moaning about my job as I love what I do, but my boyfriend Jim teases me whenever I say how exhausted I am. He really doesn't get it as he works in a call centre from nine to five, and by all accounts has it pretty cushy. He has regular lunch and tea breaks, a short bus ride to work, while I travel for over an hour each way and am lucky if I get to grab a sandwich or have a coffee, even on the quieter days.

'I am starting to feel like an unpaid servant at home, as he does absolutely nothing to help. I do the washing, the cooking, the shopping, the lot. Whenever I complain, he says I remind him of his mother who used to nag at him constantly, so I immediately stop, clam up and don't say any more, as he had a tough upbringing and I don't want to upset him.'

Jennie is 51 and owns a successful florist's in London:

'I have been married to Tom for twelve years and love him to bits and know he loves me, but he never remembers my birthday, or shows me any affection. He is obsessed with his golf and is out playing virtually every weekend and bank holiday, and I feel invisible. He never asks me about my business, and I feel really awkward bringing any of this up as he is loyal, kind and hardworking. Although it upsets me I feel I can't say anything as he will think I am being unreasonable.'

Marti is 28, an admin assistant living in Oxford:

'Since I started dating at 17, its been the same pattern around men. It's weird. They mess me about and often turn up late, or not at all. They often say things to put me down and laugh at my views on current affairs. Some have been unfaithful; many have been mean with money and remarks. I am always polite and kind and reliable, and I don't get it. However, I don't really feel comfortable saying anything, but I wondered if you could help me raise my confidence and self-esteem, then I would attract different guys, right?'

Janet is a 42-year-old entrepreneur living in Brighton:

'I am probably making a fuss about this, but I am a little confused around my boyfriend. I have been going out with Stewie for six years and about six months ago I decided to leave my job and set up a business. He was really supportive in so many ways, encouraging me to take action, making helpful suggestions, motivating and inspiring me, yet when I started to get courageous and implement some of the ideas we had discussed he made unkind remarks. He would imply that I wasn't smart enough to make the business successful, or say I couldn't raise my prices as I wasn't exactly getting clients knocking down my door with the prices I am currently charging, or that I wasn't really making much effort to market myself, so how could I expect things to take off.

'None of this was true, as I was working all hours of the day and night and also taking risks, and I found I kept defending my actions and strategies, as if he was my boss. This really affected me and slowly started to knock my confidence, as although he said these remarks gently, just thrown into conversations, I still took them to heart. When I got upset he would tell me to stop being so sensitive and that he was being helpful and supporting me, but I actually find it really upsetting and am now doubting my abilities to get this business off the ground. When I tell him these remarks upset me, he is really apologetic, saying he honestly thought he was being helpful and that they are not criticisms. He stops for about three to four weeks and is incredibly nice to me, and then starts back again. I don't want to say any more as I don't think he intends any harm, but my confidence is slipping. What should I do?'

All of these amazing women felt uneasy speaking their truth, and the longer they left it the harder it was to say anything. They are all from different backgrounds, different ages and at different stages in their life, yet they were all behaving like Doormats. People-pleasing is an epidemic, that's for sure.

Annie's solutions

I asked each one to write a letter to the person they were upset with and to remember that the point of the letter was to let go of the suppressed emotions they felt, so to be as angry as they liked and scream and shout – but do it in the letter. I encouraged them to write exactly what they felt, then to fill a bath of warm water, light a candle and burn the letter. Or they could buy a Chinese paper lantern, put the letter in the lantern and send it up into the sky. If they still felt anger it could also help to do a kick-boxing class or punch a pillow. (I asked them to ensure they kept the pillow for this purpose and then put it away somewhere, and not to use the same pillow to sleep on as it would contain all their angry energy, which is not a good thing to have around when you sleep.) I also suggested they go to an empty park early in the morning and scream out loud. Basically, that they did whatever it took to dispel any anger in a healthy way.

Next I suggested they prepared a nice supper at home for their partner, or that they went out together for coffee or a meal and, in a calm, rational tone, said:

• It hurt me when…
• I feel disrespected when…
• I am fed up with…
• It is unacceptable to speak to me that way…
• I felt it was totally inappropriate when you…
• I don't allow anyone to talk down to me.
• I deserve to be treated with respect.
• I love you, but I love me too.
• I feel angry that…
• I am disappointed you are still saying those things after I asked you to stop.

Practise, practise, practise. By practising we will become far more confident and comfortable about approaching the issue, so I asked each one of them to be prepared and look in the mirror and, in a centred way, state what it was they were upset, disappointed or angry about. We listed each issue they wanted to bring up and carefully went through each one to be sure they had clarity on exactly what was going on inside them and also to be clear on what their objective was, rather than reacting and being unreasonable. It's also important that you write a letter of forgiveness to yourself as it is essential to forgive yourself for all the times you allowed yourself to remain in an unhealthy relationship and didn't stand up for yourself.

This exercise is about 1. taking responsibility for ourselves and 2. standing up and being heard. Once we have done both of these and learnt what lessons are there and taken action, we let go and move on. If we then decide to stay with our partner, when he or she ignores our requests for respect, that is down to us – but know this, the best way to crush confidence and self-esteem is to choose to remain a Doormat and let others trample all over us.

I also gave each one of these clients an emotional freedom technique session, so they could apply this before confronting their partner in order to stay calm and centred. EFT is effective, practical and powerful and has around an eighty per cent success rate in the US. (EFT website is listed at the back of the book.)

If we meet a partner who has their own interests at heart and not ours, it's music to their ears when we go along with all that works for them and don't say anything. This set-up places us in a totally vulnerable position; they have carte blanche to dominate and control us. We are opening up the door and saying, in effect, 'Hey, good to meet you, pleased you saw the sign on the gate which says "walk all over me and tell me what is best for me, what I ought to do, tell me how to think and run my life and criticise me". I have been expecting you; come on in!' It's time to hand back your Doormat script and pick up a new one, and this new one is called 'I honour and value myself' and I make my own choices and trust my intuition.

OK, we have seen some case studies and you now get where I am coming from, so it's time to take a look at you. Below is a list of traits and I want you to get a pen and pad and start taking notes. You can also use the pages at the back of the book, but a separate notebook may be more convenient here.

Traits of Doormats

I have found that many of us have both Doormat and Diva tendencies – although your ego may not want you to admit that, but then your ego won't want you to read this book and change your mindset anyway, so I would ignore any resistance and denial and start looking at the reality of your situation.

The traits of both Doormats and Divas fall into the same four categories:

• Denial
• Low self-esteem
• Compliance
• Control

However, with the Doormat, denial, low self-esteem and *compliance* is more prominent and with the Diva, *control* is the more prominent trait. Please read this statement a few times over.

Being a Doormat can show itself in such subtle behavioural patterns, and it always amazes me how some people can be incredibly Diva-like with their work and really reach great heights as they are so forceful and full-on, yet with men they flip into being a Doormat in an instance. I have seen it many times. Some women can also be total Doormats at work and would not dream of taking the risk of running their own company, but when it comes to men they rule the roost and are complete Divas.

There is no rhyme or reason and often no logic to our behaviour. It is as it is, and I am not here to start unravelling what happened at school or in childhood in order to mould this behaviour into your present system and mindset. I am writing this book to point out the traits many people have which are causing issues with their current relationships, and/or patterns around partners, and to bring insights, tools and techniques in order to help you make changes. I have written this chapter to assist in self-evaluation and highlight what requires attention and transformation. Let's take a look at this list. Do you resonate with any of these situations?

• Suffering in silence, acting helpless and playing the martyr.
• Whining, placating and hinting (when wanting something).

- Acting ambiguously, blaming others, defending what you want.
- Denying reality, beating up on yourself.
- Giving in, over and over again, to other people's demands.
- Being dishonest by saying yes when you mean no.
- Rationalising everything.
- Standing at the back of the room with hunched shoulders.
- Constantly apologising.
- Being afraid to voice your opinion.
- Being way too nervous to ever set a boundary.
- Avoiding confrontation at all costs.
- Constantly caretaking everyone in order to be needed.
- Always needing to prove what a good person you are.
- Losing yourself when you fall in love.

Get honest

It's time to get real here. Do you ever pluck up the courage to say no and then defend your reasons, waffling on in the hope that your partner will not go off you? Do you offer help or unsolicited advice as you think that this way they will want you more? Do you feel nervous about voicing your opinion while out with your partner and their family or friends or work colleagues? If so, I hope this is making you stop and think. Remember however, that it's essential you observe your behaviour without judging yourself.

Denial

If you are in denial you will:

- Have trouble identifying what you are feeling.
- Minimise, alter and deny what you are feeling.
- Perceive yourself as dedicated to the well-being of others.
- Be uneasy receiving recognition and compliments.

Do you have a problem identifying what you feel, or if you do hit the spot with it, do you then minimise it or deny it? If so, why would you do that? What is wrong with how you feel? Who says you have to feel a certain way or at a certain time or in a certain style? Do you attach shame, or judge yourself, or make yourself into a bad person for feeling a certain way? You will hear me say this over and over throughout the book: 'it is as it is'. There is no right or wrong way to feel.

Where do you deny reality and put ear muffs on? Where are you hiding from the truth? Are you in la-la land most of the time rather than looking at what is really taking place?

• Is there something you don't want to face right now?
• OK, so what challenges have you handled successfully in the past?
• What character traits helped you handle your challenges before?

Please get your pen and pad out (or you could write here, but you may need more space) and complete these statements:

I don't want to face / I feel I am avoiding…

1 ....

2 ....

The challenges I have faced and dealt with successfully in the past were…

1 ....

2 ....

The character traits that helped me deal successfully with challenges before were…

1 ....

2 ....

Put these aside for a couple of weeks, then return to them and write down anything else that you have remembered.

Low self-esteem

When you have low self-esteem you:

• Are uneasy around asking anyone to meet your needs.
• Judge yourself harshly.
• Never feel good enough.
• Need everyone else's approval.

Are you an approval addict? Is everyone's else's opinion much more valuable than your own? Do you put others on a pedestal? Come on, own up, tell yourself the truth! Do you always feel 'less than'? Do you get uneasy at the thought of asking someone else to give you what you need? When people compliment you, do you shrug it off, thinking they are just being polite? Whatever good things happen or however successful you are, do you never quite feel good enough about yourself? Now here is where you can get honest.

My inner critic always berates me for…

1 ....

2 ....

I don't feel confident enough to ask for…

1 ....

2 ....

Often I look for other people's approval on…

1 ....

2 ....

If you think of anything else, keep writing, and in fact write and write until you get it all out. This will help you get clear on the changes that need to take place and any fears you have been avoiding looking at.

Compliance

If you are compliant, you:

• Take responsibility for everyone else's feelings.
• Accept sex when you want love.
• Are afraid to express how you feel if it differs from others.
• Compromise your integrity and values to avoid upsetting others.

Take some time and then write the most recent times these statements have been true for you. Remember this is not about berating yourself, this is a learning curve – if you don't know what the issue is, how can you move forward?

I can't say no to_____ about _____ as it would upset them:

1 ....
2 ....

I have had sex with my partner when I only wanted a hug because…

1 ....
2 ....

The reason I find it hard to express my opinion with _____
is because…

1 ....
2 ....

These lists are not all inclusive; there are many traits as each person is unique. However, I am hoping you get the picture. The point I am wanting to make is that we need to pick out what resonates with us, identify which personality traits cause us the most discomfort and then decide to do something about it.

Take a look at what isn't working

Each one of you is responsible for your own self. Once you get the responses down on paper, you gain clarity by shining a halogen light on behaviours and patterns. Awareness is the prerequisite for change.

Doormats, quite simply, do not believe they are good enough, deep down. Dress sense, conversations and body language often send out signals of 'I am not worthy'. However, the paradox here is that often some of the most powerful, beautifully dressed, slim, incredibly successful people in the world turn into Doormats when it comes to relationships. In all fairness, insecurity happens to the best of us at times. However with Doormats, insecurity remains in full-time residence.

Confident people are propelled by their insecurities; Doormats become paralysed by them. You see, as Doormats we put the needs of others before our own as a matter of habit. The craziness in this is that we can't give away what we don't have. When we feel unimportant and apologise for taking up space in the world, everyone else becomes more important, more worthy and more valuable than us and, of course, that means their needs instantly take priority.

Doormats dislike confrontation immensely; preferring to keep the peace and play the good person. Being helpful and well behaved is what Doormats pride themselves on. Often, when many finally dare to be brave and speak their truth, they immediately leap in to explain, justify or defend themselves in order that others don't think of them as being bad or selfish people.

Drop out of the 'I'm not good enough' club

This behaviour fuels our already chronic low self-esteem, and we lose respect for ourselves and lose respect from others. People actually find it irritating being around someone who faffs, can't make a decision and wants to keep pleasing everyone. It is a major turn off to many, believe me.

Here's the thing: often because as Doormats we lack the courage to be direct and ask for what we want or say what we think, some of us become manipulative, not having the confidence to ask directly for what we want and need. We then cheat ourselves out of so much.

If we walk around being a yes person, it's the same as being a servant. By hunching our shoulders, drooping down and looking inward, we are almost apologising for taking up space. By avoiding eye contact, hiding behind the truth and waffling on endlessly, rather than getting straight to the point, we are behaving like nervous children. This gives the same message as remaining silent, which means we are in fear. Did you know that according to experts, body language communicates 50% of what we really mean, the way we project our voice communicates 43% and our actual words only 7%?

This behaviour is not good. We can't wait and hope for something to change, or for safety and security within ourselves to gallop towards us. Well, we can wait, but we could be waiting for ever. One of my favourite sayings is 'Time waits for no man' – and neither does Annie!

I want to awaken you to the fact that we are all perfectly imperfect and – surprise, surprise – not everyone will love, approve of or appreciate us, but that's OK. However, it is helpful to remember that if we don't confront others, it infers that we are putting ourselves down, as in essence we are agreeing with other people. It is vital to add that there is a huge difference between berating ourselves and taking responsibility for ourselves. Everybody is entitled to their own views, opinions and preferences. We don't need to drop our integrity in order to people-please. Why would we do that as it's exhausting and, quite honestly, fake and ridiculous? After all, how would we ever be truly able to please every single person we encountered? Learning to champion ourselves is fun, feels great and will bring us oodles of self-approval.

Not everyone can always be expected to be there for us, so we have to learn to stand on our own two feet. Saying that, it's not about being self-centred either, or renewing our membership to www.me-me-me. com. Not all men are princes and not all women are princesses, and no one can guarantee a happily ever after, fairy-tale relationship. We have to focus on extreme self-care and be self-reliant at times.

Remember, we all deserve to be treated with respect and kindness, and if we settle for less, we will always get less than we settled for. Where is the point in acting in a sneaky way? Why not grow our courage muscles and face people head on? After all, what is the worst that can happen? Why not swap mumbling for speaking clearly and with distinction? Sadly, many people reinforce their situation by behaving in a manner that encourages others to distrust them. You need to always be aware that your verbal and non-verbal behaviour plays a huge role in your relationships and well-being. Running around town like an eager beaver desperately telling others what they want to hear in order to avoid any conflict is so last season, and utterly fake.

Stop for a moment and have a think. Why do people often do this? Are we nervous of showing our anger? Are we feeling the need to hide any hostility and be all sugar and spice towards people we don't like? Who is holding a weapon to our head to insist we behave in a certain way when we don't want to? Are we ignoring alert signs because we feel uncomfortable confronting our partner about the way they spoke to us in front of our family, or fearful to be open and admit we don't fancy them anymore, or are we unhappy with the fact we found lipstick on a shirt collar? Or is it about feeling taken for granted by always being the one doing the school run, or paying for everything? Or what about feeling irritated at being the one getting up in the middle of the night to feed the baby, or always the one to forfeit having a drink as someone has to remain sober to drive home after an evening out? How about feeling sick and tired of always being kept waiting?

By saying nothing, all that happens is that we remain dishonest and act contrary to our feelings and words, and enable the person we need to confront to continue upsetting and disrespecting us. We can pretend to not notice, avoid confrontation and keep the peace in order to not take a risk, but why would we do that?

It's time to make changes

By taking an informed risk we change our internal talk from 'I feel used and taken for granted, I am tired of people taking advantage, I am being disrespected' to 'I feel powerful, I am worthy, I am in control and I feel confident'.

If you recognise any of these traits and continue to enable someone to take advantage, perhaps your underlying issue is that of feeling worthless. If this nonsense keeps running the show, I urge you to make a commitment to yourself *today* to make changes. If you are single, surrender the role of the Doormat before diving headlong into the next relationship hungry for love and willing to tolerate humiliation and emotional torture. Leave the Doormat dance behind and start slowly, a step at a time, taking action to change your behaviour. If you are in a relationship, and feel nervous of changing the dynamics, you need to be courageous and know that by starting to honour yourself your relationship will improve dramatically. It will become way more open and honest, that's for sure. We have to be willing to observe what we are doing and not doing, and monitor the results that are showing up in our life and in our relationships.

In order to make changes and to move forward we have to firstly begin with an honest self-diagnosis. I used to pride myself on being the rock for everyone else. My need to be needed was so deep. I wanted to be liked at any cost; I needed to tap-dance around for affirmation constantly in order to receive approval. However, I soon learnt that the more I looked for approval the less I received. The less I looked for it, the more I received.

Many clients tell me they really believe the only way they will be invited out and included in another person's life is to do everything the other person wants. Many of us women constantly give away what we don't have: time, energy, money, love, whatever. We give and give as we are convinced that will guarantee us being loved or liked.

Many of us allow others' expectations, demands, agendas, needs and issues to control us. We possess a deep fear of being alone, and worry that other people will not accept us. The thing is, when we behave like a Doormat and don't take care of ourselves, we immediately give other people permission to have control over us.

It isn't our job to run around taking care of everyone else and constantly worrying about their reaction if we speak up. We are a hundred per cent responsible for ourselves. Sure, we can be kind and offer support, love, and a listening ear and friendship. But if we neglect ourselves and don't give to ourselves, how can we give anything to others? Anyway, what will be left to give, as we will be depleted? If we don't love and respect ourselves, how can we expect others to do so? Time to give up the Doormat role. We are worthwhile, so we must enjoy, embrace and celebrate that. Even if we haven't waxed our legs in a while, have put on a few pounds or haven't had our roots done for ages, we are still amazing just as we are.

None of the above reasons make it OK for anybody to treat us with anything less than the utmost respect we deserve. It is amazing how others are drawn to us when we accept ourselves. Once we accept our assets and our flaws, we send out an energy which is incredibly attractive.

Now, some of you may not have been given much love and affection as children, while others may have had lots. Either way, this does not make you unlovable, so it's good to make that a mantra and tell yourself a thousand times a day 'I am more than enough exactly as I am'.

Let's meet Jeannie

Jeannie is fabulous and came to me for a mix of Emotional Freedom Technique and coaching to bust some old beliefs about not feeling good enough. She was fed up with not sustaining long-term relationships. She is 35 and recently set up her own business. She is also bright, funny, open-minded, enthusiastic about life and very social. Jeannie is attracted to men who are professional, wealthy, handsome and charming and a few years older than her – so, you may think, what's the big deal? There's nothing surprising with the type of guys she fancies, but the problem is that she goes from being a confident businesswoman to a complete Doormat with men. Let's look at an example of a situation she experienced just before our first session.

'Paul and I have been dating for eight months; he's good looking, and I really like him. He is a successful property developer, witty, charming, great in bed and generous. He called me one weekday lunchtime saying he had a client arriving from the States that afternoon who he was taking out for dinner at 7.00 p.m. He wanted me to accompany them – don't get me wrong, I loved that he wanted to include me – but I had a bad headache and hadn't slept much the night before as I was on a deadline with a project and getting really stressed. I had tons of work still to do, and had planned to work through until about 8.00 p.m. and then go home, have a hot bath and try to catch up with sleep by hitting my bed by 10.00 at the latest. Paul said it was essential I looked the part, as this guy was mega-important. No pressure, then… I just couldn't find the courage to say no, so I explained about my deadline, being sure he would understand (as he's self-employed too), but he just spoke over me. I felt angry and invisible, but still couldn't find the strength to say no. He is so seductive and charming that I find him hard to resist. I explained I wasn't dressed appropriately for a posh venue, and wouldn't have time to go home and change.

'I started feeling really pressured and flustered as he wouldn't hear any of it, and just kept telling me this guy was an important client and if I cared about him I would go, and why was I being selfish? I do love him and I am sure he loves me, so I raced off to Covent Garden and bombed about in the rain, and of course as I had left the office in such a hurry, I hadn't taken an umbrella, so my hair was now all frizzy. I couldn't find any shoes, but I did spot a dress in the first shop I went into, and it was perfect, so I bought that and then raced to a couple of shoe shops and begrudgingly bought shoes I couldn't afford and didn't need, and then realised I needed to go get a blow-dry but was short on time, so I bought some hair straighteners and was thinking what are you doing, you have some at home… I started feeling a bit ratty at this point and so I jumped in a cab back to the office before doing my credit card any more damage, grabbed a coffee and got back to work. It was about 4.00 p.m. before I realised I hadn't even bought a salad or sandwich for lunch. I had run out of headache tablets and my head was thumping.

'I felt so bummed out. I was tired, stressed and had loads to do for my deadline, and all I wanted was to crawl into my bed and sleep. Then a little voice kept saying "the show must go on" and I get that, but it wasn't my show. At 6.00 p.m. I changed in the tiny toilet at the office, gulped another cup of coffee, slapped some make-up on and raced out to find a taxi.'

When she recalled this story to me, Jeannie was feeling resentful: it wasn't the first time this had happened. I asked her what she wished she had done. She got upset and said she had been so used to putting men's needs first and neglecting herself that she wasn't sure how she could have handled it any differently. Whenever she did feel she should say something, she felt guilty and went back to her autopilot response, which was 'I can't say no'. I must please him.

Annie's solutions

I explained that it would have been powerful not to have backed down with her plans of working on her deadline and hitting the sack at 10.00 p.m. This way Paul might think twice before calling her at such short notice and expecting her to jump; it would teach him how to treat her. I also explained that if she did want to be impulsive and go along with his plans, then that was fine too. This is about what truly works for her and not about abandoning herself in fear of Paul abandoning her. Anyone worth their salt would not consider dropping her or sulking because she didn't slide into what they want every time they wanted it. The people that matter don't mind, and the people who mind don't matter.

Choices

Jeannie had choices, but admits she didn't think she did. Firstly, when Paul suggested the meal that night with his client, she could 'accept to decline'. She had always allowed men to ring her at the last minute and call the shots and she always went along with it, almost automatically.

She could have broken that pattern by:

- Explaining that as much as she would like to go, she had a deadline to meet.
- Stating that she preferred more notice, especially when it was such an important dinner.
- Suggesting they went somewhere more casual so she didn't have to change.
- Suggesting Paul changed the booking to later in order to give her a chance to go home, have a shower and change her clothes.
- Suggesting she joined them for a pre-drink (or perhaps a coffee after the meal, had that been possible).

Any one of these responses would have doubled her confidence, but by dropping into her Doormat default setting, her confidence and self-esteem plummeted. She freely admitted that the only thing on her mind was doing what Paul wanted. She became invisible; she didn't feel she had the right to question him. Her low self-esteem told her she was lucky to have such an amazing boyfriend, and the constant committee in her head told her that in order to keep him she must do what he wanted, as then he would love her more and never leave her. Until we started the sessions, she told me that when anyone remarked that Paul was really self-centred, she would go into total denial and make all sorts of excuses for him, defending him all the way. Her ear muffs would stay firmly on her ears.

So what happened that night?

'Well, I turned up on time looking smart and Paul introduced me to his client. He never made any remark about how I looked or that he was pleased I could make it, or asked how my deadline was coming along. He never said much to me, actually; they talked all through the meal about business and, to be honest, I felt I could have been a cardboard cut-out. I was so angry. At 11.00 p.m. we all said goodnight, and Paul said he had a 7.00 a.m. meeting and needed to sleep and dashed off home without even thinking about ordering me a taxi. This is always how it's been, but for some reason I suddenly got it. Something snapped inside me, which is why I decided to have a session with you as I didn't know how to make changes.'

Jeannie had no self-respect when it came to men, and no confidence to say anything. This is not about blaming Paul. He is only going along with what he can get away with, and it would have been no good pointing the finger of blame at him, or shouting or screaming at him. Jeannie needed to leave the role of Doormat behind – and she was finally realising it.

Jeannie says:
'I left Paul some weeks later. When the dynamics changed, with me using new techniques and tools and my confidence growing, he sadly didn't like the new me. It suited him just fine to have the old Jeannie. I was really upset for a few months, but refused to give in to him trying to coax me back into my old ways. Now, six months on, I have just started dating a guy called Roy I met at a networking event, although I wasn't in any way looking for anyone. He has the utmost respect for me and it's a totally different feeling as Roy loves the fact I am so confident and speak up for myself. He says he feels so proud to be dating someone so confident. Sometimes I slip back into my old behaviour, but I always get myself back on track really quickly, as nothing and no one will ever be able to get me back behaving like a Doormat again. I did beat myself up for a while when Paul and I finished as it hit me hard how much of a pushover I had been all these years. Annie really supported me through this with hypnotherapy sessions, planting loads of powerful affirmations in my subconscious. I did the best I could with the knowledge I had at the time and it was crucial to forgive myself. We did a lot of sessions around forgiving myself and letting go, and I cried a lot, and things really started shifting. Then we had motivational hypnotherapy sessions, which were really powerful in building up my confidence and self-esteem, and Annie gave me affirmations to say over and over. She kept reminding me that if I had known differently, I would have done differently. I am so grateful to have these tools and a new-found self-confidence, as not only have I found a new partner who treats me with respect, but I now respect myself and because of that lots of things have improved for me.'

Reflection

Take responsibility. You must show other people that you are valuable and worth respecting. Step away from operating from fear, low self-esteem and neediness. Start again on a new footing, one coming from courage, faith and confidence in yourself. This is much better. Take other people off the pedestal you have placed them on, and put yourself there instead. Stop expending so much energy worrying about what will happen if you stand up for yourself? **Just do it.**

Be yourself. Practise saying 'I love you, but I love me too'. Only controlling people want you to agree with their every word and act like a robot. Why would you want to be involved with a controlling person? Why would you want to be a robot? Healthy people respect someone who has an opinion and is not afraid to voice it; no one respects anybody who allows themselves to be dominated and controlled. Who respects a Doormat? Let's get real; Doormats are there to be walked upon. Sorry if that sounds harsh, but it's the reality. Later on, we'll look at communication skills and techniques to combat this Doormat behaviour.

You are more than enough exactly as you are. You must not let anyone tell you otherwise. You must not allow anyone to dishonour you. You can carry on with low self-esteem and no inner confidence and allow others to decide your destiny, or you can say 'I'm done. I now choose to do what is in my best interest'. It's entirely up to you.

Question

What action are you willing to take today in order to give up the role of Doormat?

Action

Get hold of George Michael's Album Patience and play the track 'I think you're amazing', and play it loud, over and over again. Change 'you're' to 'I'm' and sing it at the top of your voice every day for a week, dancing in front of a mirror. Repeat this like a mantra daily. Maybe you don't like George Michael but do it anyway; go girl!

2 Am I a Diva?

Unsolicited advice is worthless because it hasn't been requested

You may be curious to know what a Diva's traits are. Well, they are very similar to those of a Doormat in some ways, as both stem from low self-esteem and ego. When we are acting from our ego, we are acting from a place of 'better than others' or 'less than others' – and, either way, the reality is that we don't feel great about ourselves, which in turn means we have low levels of confidence.

In the previous chapter we looked at denial, low self-esteem, compliance and control and, if you recall, I stated that compliance was more prominent in a Doormat and control was more prominent in a Diva.

We are therefore going to focus in this chapter on denial, low self-esteem and control. Remember when we want to be in control of everybody and everything, we are behaving in a self-centred and selfish manner, as our prime concern is always to take care of ourselves, regardless of anyone or anything else. Now, this topic is multilayered and pretty complex, so I will keep it as simple and succinct as possible. A Diva is often a control freak, but many disguise their controlling traits by being charming yet manipulative – so if being seduced by a Diva, always bear this in mind. They have their best interests at heart, not anybody else's.

However, if you are a Diva, please take a step back and look at how self-centred you are being, much as it may pain your ego to admit it. When you read the following clients' 'dating Diva' stories you will see how Divas like to manipulate other people by rescuing them and doing things they haven't asked for so they become indebted and feel obligated. Divas like to shame other people and blame them.

Keith's dating Diva

Keith, an IT manager from Bath, is 36 and was dating Sally, a 34-year-old hairdresser from London. This is what he said:

'I decided to knock it on the head with Sally after a few months, as although she was hot and there was a lot of physical attraction, she non-stop moaned. I asked her about her work when we met, and she spent twenty minutes complaining about everyone and pointing out everyone's shortcomings, and seemed to have an opinion on everything. It wasn't just her cynicism and negative attitude that turned me off, it was her expectation that everyone ought to be doing what she thought was best. I started seeing a real Diva in her which I found so unattractive. I didn't like the way she spoke to waiters and to staff as it was more demanding than requesting, and it amazed me that she could never see she had any faults. She sulked if we didn't do what she wanted and acted like a child. I used to drive up to London every weekend to see her – fair enough; I didn't mind – but I felt irked after the first month of dating as she made it clear that she just expected me to. Whatever I did for her, like plan a nice meal somewhere or book tickets for the theatre, she just took for granted. Not once did she offer to pay for anything. Don't get me wrong, I earn a fair amount of money and enjoyed spoiling her, but if she had offered it would have meant so much. But it really had nothing to do with money, it was her attitude that I felt stank.

'I also struggled with her telling me what I ought to wear and advising me on my work, and telling me what the best way was to get fit and what I ought to eat, and how I ought to be drinking wine instead of beer. I felt like her son rather than her partner, and I found it really offensive rather than helpful or caring. My life had been running very well before we met, work-wise and fitness-wise, so that really did irritate me. Also if I promised to call and rang later than I said I would or arrived late at her place on a Friday night due to traffic, she would be aloof or angry, which I don't find alluring at all. If I went out with the boys and forgot to call her, she would play games, such as not returning my call the next night or saying something to try and make me jealous. Now I realise that it was the sex that kept us together; I think she knew this as when I pulled back she always used sex to hook me in and I fell for it each time. In all honesty, I don't think I have ever come across anyone so childlike, manipulative and self-absorbed.'

Jenny's dating Diva

Jenny says:
'I met Raf when we were working at an events company in Leeds, where we both live. He was 32 and I was 35. He was funny, charming and generous and we got along from the start. He often poked fun at me at work, but I used to laugh and shrug it off. However, after a few months we ended up smooching at the end of one of the events our company had organised which was way out of line, as our management were around. It was late and we had a couple of glasses of bubbly and neither of us had eaten all evening, and before I knew it he had ordered us both a cab and we were on our way to a club. One thing led to another and he ended up crashing back at my place. The next morning felt slightly awkward but we had a shower, got it together and, agreeing we both felt like death warmed up and needed a stimulant, headed off to Starbucks where we grabbed a cappuccino, a double espresso and two skinny muffins and ran for the bus to get to the office. A few days went by and we didn't speak about what had happened, and then Raf called me on the Friday at about 10.00 p.m., sounding a bit worse for wear and asked me out on a date.

'We arranged to meet on the Sunday evening at a local brasserie. It was a lovely balmy June evening and we were given a table outside. We had a great meal and a lot of laughs, and he was very complimentary. He championed me when I said my dream was to open up my own bakery, making bespoke cup-cakes and pastries. I rarely shared my dreams with anyone, but the warm sun on my back and giddiness in my head after my fourth glass of Chardonnay meant I found my nerve and let my words do their own thing without restriction. We started dating. To begin with we saw each other most nights; he made me feel special and was very supportive when I started gabbling away at night, telling him about information I had acquired about government funding for new businesses.

'About ten months into the relationship he started putting me down and making snide remarks. When I said that these remarks upset me, he would always say he was joking, and that I should stop being so precious. I always ended up apologising to him as he had the knack of making me feel guilty. Then we would go out, get drunk and he would seduce me with his charm and wit and I would forgive him – every time.

'Then I came to see Annie for coaching around setting up my business and she asked me various questions, one of which was whether I had support from friends and my partner. It hit me like a ton of bricks that I didn't. In fact, my friends said I was nuts and Raf wasn't supporting me; he was crushing my confidence and in truth belittling my dreams. Annie asked me to describe some typical remarks, and I did. Then she explained that it's often people who are insecure who do this so they can feel superior. She also explained that many people like to control others as their self-inflated ego always tells them that they know best.

'After that session, something snapped and I decided to tackle Raf. I asked him why he always had to have an opinion on everything, and why he felt he knew best about my business, my lifestyle, my goals. He was pretty shocked at my outburst, as I had always gone along with everything he said. However, he told me he was giving me advice as he wanted what was best for me. I asked him why he thought he knew what was best for me, and what qualified him to give me business advice when he had only ever been a wage slave. I know that is a cruel thing to say, but I was so angry and had enough with his put-downs and sulking when I didn't follow his advice. However, having spoken with Annie I realised that it wasn't about me, it was about his control issues. Though he might appear fun, together and confident to the outside world, a layer of deep insecurity, resentment and anger was lurking underneath.

'Now that Annie had helped me to have the courage to confront him on his behaviour, my confidence and self-esteem really started rocketing. The following month I left Raf, and three months later handed in my notice and started supplying my cakes to outlets. It's going really well; I feel completely different about myself and life feels amazing.'

Robin and Janine the Diva

Robin says:
'I was always shy as a youngster and chose to suffer in silence with many challenging situations at home and at school. Looking back, I realise I had such low self-esteem and low self-worth. I was living in London with my parents and younger brother, and we continually suffered through my father's alcoholism. My father tried to get me arrested, provoked both me and my brother endlessly, and I learnt to become aggressive with my reactions in order to protect myself and cover up my fear. When I was only 9, my father threatened to kill me, my brother and mother and we all locked ourselves in the kitchen. I remember vividly seeing the blade of a knife coming through the door, with my father ranting and raving. I grew up on edge, always walking on eggshells, nervous of upsetting my father. When I was 14 my father tried to kill my mother; she raced up the stairs, and I was in between them trying with all my might to protect my mother. My father was so drunk he lost his balance and the knife went through the banister, just missing her.

'I grew up with such an aggressive father that I had no idea what boundaries were and the only reaction I knew how to give was an aggressive one. When I started university I stayed at home in order to protect my mother, and continued to play the mediator. I had no girlfriends and no social life and my life was very small really. By the time I reached 20, I was short-changing myself in every area. I never asked for my needs to be met or ever asked for what I wanted. I never believed I deserved anything good to happen to me. I squashed all my needs and put everyone else's feelings before mine. I was always the good guy, the nice guy, never doing anything out of place. Doubt and fear reigned in me, and although I succeeded with building myself up physically and going that extra mile with pushing my body, I was unable to do that with my mind. I was very loyal in every work situation and made personal sacrifices for the sake of the job. It was always about getting it right and being liked than looking pragmatically at the facts. I always allowed other people to abuse me and trample on me and just couldn't be assertive.

'When I was 28 I met Janine. I really fell for her, even though she had an aggressive attitude and never considered anyone else's needs or desires, including mine. She was pretty, slim, bright and witty and we instantly hit it off. Looking back, I can now see where her character traits (which were disguised initially by charm) were similar to my father's. She was insensitive, greedy, hugely self-centred, hypocritical, and she had a massive ego. In simple terms, she was a real bully. Conflicting thoughts went through my head continually. Firstly, Janine took advantage of my kind nature and the fact I wasn't assertive; secondly, she never appeared to appreciate the time and energy I put into trying to make her happy. Somehow I convinced myself that she did appreciate me, but couldn't show it and that it was fine to make sacrifices in a relationship. I felt a mixture of shame and anger at myself for tolerating her behaviour. It took me a while to decide to leave – in fact, it was when I went to see Annie and she asked me why I was allowing Janine to hold me in bondage in order for her to feel good about herself that something snapped inside me. That was the moment I decided to walk away.'

Megan's Diva partner

Megan says:
'I find it really challenging that Sharon is always insistent that she organises everything and then complains. It's got to the point where I am afraid to let her do anything as I know she will keep score and keep track of everything. Often I get home from work on a Friday and she will complain she has done all the housework, fetched the food from the supermarket, prepared supper, and on and on. I always explain I would have been quite happy to have done the housework

on Saturday morning, and also I'm very happy to pick up a take-away on the way home or prepare food when I get in. Then she tells me I am ungrateful and it drives me potty, as I am realising what a total control freak she is, just like my mother. She insists everything is done to her standard and on her terms, yet complains she is the one doing everything. I just don't get that.

'She is always totally convinced she is right about everything; she refuses to see my side of the story, or anybody else's. I feel a real sucker as I always end up being the one to apologise although I haven't done anything wrong – I grew up in a household full of arguments so I hate confrontations and a bad atmosphere, and end up apologising. That means she stops sulking and ranting and trying to prove her point. She is still not speaking to her brother due to something that happened way back when; she isn't speaking to her cousin because of a silly incident that took place on holiday one year; she isn't speaking to a colleague at work because of a disagreement they had over a new acquisition they were all working on. Now I've had some sessions with Annie I am realising just how crazy this whole situation is and asking myself why I tolerate it. I have to walk around on eggshells at home, which is ridiculous as we pay equal rent and contributions. If I do everything her way, she is a dream partner – but if I don't play her game or go along with what she wants, it's pretty uncomfortable. So I tend to give in but, as Annie rightly said to me, at what price to my sanity?'

As Divas, we believe deep down that we are nothing and are therefore on a constant treadmill of being useful and trotting around barking orders, insisting we know best. If you are one of these people, you need to realise that if you feel you have to prove how smart you are all the time, you are coming from a place of low self-worth.

Showing how much we are needed, how useful we are, how smart we are allows others to become dependent on us – so we can then prove our self-worth. This is crazy logic. If we are trying to create anything in our life in order to prove something, it implies doubt. When we have doubt, we are operating from a position of fear. The ego will always tell us that we are not good enough and have to prove our worth, and that we must strive for more, do better. It's purely a smokescreen keeping us away from having serenity and peace within ourselves. If we stop and listen to ourselves, we can hear the spirit gently saying 'You are more than enough as you are'. Why don't we listen?

Trying to change everyone else and tell them what they ought to be doing is what co-dependency is all about. Every time we judge others, we are actually judging ourselves. How amazing the world would be if people were willing to laugh at their self-beliefs and not take everything so personally or so seriously. After all, everyone has a right to their own take on things, and we can respect their ideologies without having to agree with them or ridiculing them.

If you go around constantly offering unsolicited advice, you are saying 'I need you to need me so I can start feeling good about myself; please need me…'

Acts of kindness are only kind when we feel good about ourselves. Caretaking is the neighbour of martyrdom.

Divas often have a compulsion to be perfect. I found being a Diva exhausting; I was trying to be the perfect woman and being a master of the universe was a full-time job. We don't have to be perfect to get someone to love us. It's insanity to think that. It does help, however, to have a sense of humour, good communication skills, self-approval – and to lighten up and take our nose out of everyone else's life and focus on our own instead.

Take a pen and pad, use this space or the pages at the end of the book. You can have more than two answers to these questions, of course…

Who irritates you the most? What qualities about them most irritate you?

1 ....

2 ....

Whom do you judge the most, and for what behaviour?

1 ....

2 ....

What quality do you deny in yourself which you can see so clearly in others?

1 ....

2 ....

What hurts you the most when someone accuses you of being like it? (for example, being selfish, angry, insensitive, mean, and so forth)

1 ....

2 ....

What do you feel shame around being or doing?

1 ....

2 ....

There is no point answering these unless you are vigorously honest. Take your time and know that these answers will give you greater insights into the shadow parts you may not currently be owning.

Each week, pick someone who triggers you, winds you up or irritates you, and observe them without judging them. Ask yourself this: 'If I was totally being myself, what would I say?'

When we sit in judgment, we are sitting in a pool of resistance, and whatever we resist will persist. If we can accept and embrace all our judgments, things in our life will change. All that we don't like about ourselves we project onto others and dump on them – not very nice! Many people cope with the rejected parts of themselves by labelling themselves as bad and stupid, and their inner critic goes overboard and then they accord these labels to others. They think like this: 'If I make you feel bad about yourself, I will feel good about myself, and I need you to feel bad about yourself, as then I don't have to deal with the way I feel about myself.'

The reason I asked you to be honest and sit down and write answers to the questions above is because doing so makes it easy to identify what you have turned into your own darkness by judging others on what you can't stand in them.

Do any of the earlier stories about those dating Divas resonate with you? Always remember, when you encounter anything in your relationship you are not happy about, you have choices. You need to get alert as from today on your own needs and wants; stop focusing on the faults of your partner. Learn what is right, not *who* is right; this isn't a competition. Keep your nose out of your partner's issues and challenges until he or she invites you in by asking your opinion. Losers blame other people; winners take full responsibility for their actions and the consequences. Divas love to take other people hostage and demand exclusive air time without a commercial break. Why do Divas reckon other people are so interested in all the opinions they enforce?

Divas don't get mileage out of equanimity; they win only if they succeed in irritating the other person. Often the Diva's constant lecturing overcompensates for feeling emotionally abandoned and not heard as a child. Divas often nag, shout, demand, play power trips, dictate, command, moan, sulk, provoke, gossip, manipulate, control, accuse and use a variety of other methods to get their own way, like seduction techniques and issuing ultimatums. Divas are deceptive, conniving and will let nothing stop them from getting what they want. The truth is that yelling, bad-mouthing, nagging, demanding and sulking will do nothing but push a partner away.

We have choices if we are involved with someone who constantly finds fault:

- Exhaust ourselves by fighting back on every single remark and get into battle, inviting our ego to converse with their ego, and going around and around in circles.
- Ignore what's being said, don't get rattled and stop complaining.
- Leave the relationship.
- Get relationship therapy.
- Start practising being assertive.

If you are the one who is behaving like a Diva, I recommend seeing a therapist or a coach. Work on busting your ego and learning how to raise your confidence so you can quit needing to be right, begin to accept every part of yourself, and so learn to accept others as they are.

Reflection

It is crucial for you to think about how many times a day you tell other people what to do. I constantly hear people criticising others – it's incredible – and I wonder if they are doing it because they truly believe they are better. In these situations, what they are really saying is that they are superior and others are inferior.

Question

How do you react when others tell you what to do?

Action

There is a lot of power in the spoken word, so from today I suggest you become more aware of what you say and what your reactions to other people are.

3 Bye, Doormat; hello, Ms Assertive

What other people think of us is none of our business; what we think of them is none of their business

Suzie walked into our third session and said immediately 'I don't think I can see Tim any more. I feel exhausted with constantly bending myself like a pretzel for him.

After our last session I went to Starbucks, ordered a latte, sat down and burst out crying, as it just struck me like a ton of bricks that I've been trying to please everyone all my life, and I can't do it any more. I've never believed I was enough. I felt I had to make everyone like me, so I have spent years needing others to validate me. I've put so much into every relationship as a way of trying to prove what a nice person I am, doing everything they have wanted me to do. Something you said in our last session made me realise I hadn't ever believed someone could love me for me and now I'm really angry as I feel l have been walking about all these years with "mug" written on my forehead.'

I was totally flabbergasted. Much as I liked Suzie, the last couple of sessions had been challenging as she had fixed views and there was a lot of denial going on. When I'd asked if she would be willing to look at things in a slightly different way she had become defiant and resistant, and I had questioned whether she would continue with the sessions. So to hear this was a complete breakthrough; in fact, it was music to my ears. 'What was it I said that gave you this insight?' I asked.

'We were talking about Tim and you suddenly asked if I had happy memories of school. I thought that was a bizarre thing to ask. No disrespect, but I mean it was way back and, sure, girls at school made bitchy remarks; that's just the way it was. Then I remembered someone in my class who was tall, pretty and slim, and all the boys fancied her. She had short blonde hair and blue eyes, really naturally stunning. She kept calling me shortarse and fatty and everyone else in her gang would giggle. Then you asked if this had upset me, and if I'd ever answered back, and I said no. But after the session I burst out crying and it just dawned on me I was 12, maybe 13 years old and, OK, I was quite short compared to the other girls, a little overweight, but that was no reason for her to keep picking on me. Why didn't I tell the teacher, or stand up to her? One day I walked past her at the end of break and she whispered in my ear "No one will ever fancy a midget with a big arse, so get used to it."'

I asked Suzie how she felt when she had that 'ah ha' moment in Starbucks. She said, 'Tearful and upset initially that it had happened, then anger towards her for picking on me, then rage at myself for having allowed it to happen.'

During this third session Suzie was really beating herself up over it, so I asked 'Would you get away with speaking to a friend the way you speak to yourself?' She immediately said that she wouldn't, so I went on. 'Then why speak to yourself in such a punishing and cruel way?'

I explained that she'd behaved at school the only way she knew how; if she had known anything different she would have behaved differently. So she needed to give herself a break and, after all, what could be gained by bashing herself up? 'The reality is,' I said, 'we get it when we get it and "it is as it is".'

Let's meet Suzie

Let me give you a little background on Suzie. She is 32, petite, pretty and slim. She is a part-time model and shares a flat with a close girlfriend in Bayswater. Due to her deep-rooted insecurity she would not be seen dead without her Chanel shades and Jimmy Choos; image is everything to Suzie, who models herself on Cheryl Cole. She loves being seen in Chinawhite and Cloud 23 Bar at the Hilton and is a real fashionista. She has regular facials and won't go anywhere without ensuring her hair and nails are immaculate.

But when Suzie gets involved with a guy she walks out on herself and feels a constant need to prove how smart, gorgeous and desirable she is. She makes each man her project. She sends cards, notes and brownies and even packs of Vitamin C to the office if he has a cold. You see, she doesn't want him to forget her and wants to constantly convey that she likes him. Suzie's pattern is that if a guy starts to lose interest she becomes needy, and tries even harder to get his attention as she feels insecure in case he doesn't fancy her any more. When he slowly moves away from her she gets really upset and can't understand why he won't commit to her. She doesn't stand up for herself, and she doesn't say what she means or means what she says. There is no way in a million years that Suzie would ever confront a man and ask what was going on. She is so emotionally dependent on the man she is with; she needs him, so she buries her head in the sand and tries even harder to win his approval.

First session

In our first session she was tearful and anxious because her flatmate had just become engaged and was planning to get married and move abroad. She was really close friends with her flatmate and they spent a lot of time together, many evenings curled up on the sofa watching *American Idol*, discussing men, sex and what was going on with mutual friends. They went away together regularly on holiday and spoke several times a day on the phone. Now Suzie felt rejected and lonely and loads of emotions had bubbled up to the surface. Her friend Jan had been a client of mine way back and suggested that Suzie come and see me too.

Suzie also complained that her boyfriend Tim had cooled off big time and was being weird about her flatmate's engagement. She said he shared no interest in her discussing it or hearing about the wedding plans, and in fact rarely came to the flat any more. I asked her how she was handling this and she said she had bought him a couple of CDs and called to tell she loved him. He has never told her he loves her, but then that's just Tim, she said: 'he is pretty laid back'.

Tim separated from his wife three years ago after being married for eight years and has said he wasn't looking for a commitment, but Suzie doesn't believe him. She is convinced he will eventually change his mind and commit. I asked if he knew she wanted a commitment. 'Don't know,' she replied. 'I would never tell him I did as that would freak him out. He hasn't even mentioned getting a divorce and I don't like to ask why he hasn't filed for one, as I may appear desperate or needy and scare him off.' Meanwhile, she told me, she thinks it's best that she doesn't complain or make a fuss, because then he will eventually see that she is the one who will make him happy and suggest they move in together or make some kind of plans for their future.

She says he is different to all the others, as he treats her with respect. I asked her in what way and she responded 'In the way no one else has; he opens car doors, he compliments me on what I wear, compliments my humour and cooks me supper when I'm at his place.' She went on to say that he did like to get his own way with where they went to eat, what movie or TV programme they watched and what music they listened to in the car, and she does work around his schedule of rugby training, boys' nights out, weekends away with his old university mates. In fact, she said (while laughing) that he'd told her his mother had said to his ex-mother-in-law that as much as she loved her son, he was 'me-centric', and she thought any woman would need to be a saint to put up with him.

Suzie was at an event when she first set eyes on Tim and said she really fancied him. She said she felt immediately drawn to him and sensed he was dynamic and passionate, self-assured and confident. Within a few minutes she caught him looking straight at her and then within a second he was heading towards her. Wham – before she knew it they were chatting and it had all happened so quickly.

Suzie says that after several dates she had niggling doubts about taking it further. Tim didn't say as much, but she was concerned he might still be into his ex-wife; however, like everything else in life she doesn't want to hear, she put her ear muffs on and ignored it. During the eleven months they had been together since then she had kept up a façade that all was OK when in fact it wasn't. The bottom line was that Suzie wanted some sort of sign from Tim that he would commit and take their relationship seriously.

Suzie's Doormat traits need highlighting as they are traits she shares with many people. My client base is diverse, and over the past ten years I have coached a variety of people including single parents, mature students, celebrities, lawyers, writers, teachers, accountants, diplomats, secretaries, producers, architects, nurses, lecturers, bankers, admin assistants, other coaches, entrepreneurs, teens, osteopaths, graphic designers, sales assistants, singers, complementary therapists and more, and it doesn't matter what anybody does for a living or what they earn, 85% of them have the same traits disguised in different packaging. They all fall into the category of Doormat or Diva.

- Josie said she didn't feel she could push it with Toby when he said he would leave his wife and family.
- Martha didn't like to bring it up with Jake that he always promised to quit working 24/7 and spend more time with her and the children but did nothing about it.
- Jane definitely felt uneasy pulling Martin up when he picked fault with everything she wore, everything she said and constantly criticised her family and friends.
- Mitch adored Tom and Tom assured Mitch he would never hit on one of their friends again, until Mitch found out that Tom had made a pass at their mutual friend Bruce at Mitch's birthday – but Mitch said Bruce instigated it and nothing took place.
- Sandra felt she was being unreasonable if she said to Mark that she felt invisible as he never stopped talking about himself.
- Bea said Trevor was reserved and accepted that he never wanted to discuss anything with her, but preferred to roll up a joint each night in front of the TV.

- Kath felt Alan might have been a bit out of order turning up at her office party drunk and unshaven but she didn't want to upset him by saying anything.
- Chris couldn't understand why Lindsey got so angry when he told her how she should spend her money.
- Helen didn't feel it was fair that Toby should contribute financially to anything in their flat or when they went out; after all, he had several really expensive hobbies to maintain.
- Megan said Rick was only teasing when he put her down or told her she was fat; he didn't really mean it.
- Jenny knew the affair Mick had was because he was feeling upset over his father's death and it was a one-off.
- Teresa couldn't understand why Josh got so defiant when she told him how to bring up Millie, his 5-year-old daughter from his previous relationship.
- Michael didn't feel he could let Rebecca know he was really unhappy about having her mother live with them as her mother was having a hard time.
- Karina said Colin has only hit her once, when he was drunk, and he only drinks three vodkas a night as opposed to his usual six, so she can't say anything as she knows he is trying to change.

I have heard it all, over and over again. Let me make it clear that I'm not judging or criticising, I am making observations.

It's been incredible for me to have had the privilege of working with many amazing clients and watching them grow and develop and change their mindsets, making vast improvements and bringing happiness and transformation to their lives. With the combination of my personal experience (being both a recovered Diva and Doormat) and simple yet effective techniques, tools, tips and a highly trained intuition I am able to introduce a doorway, open it and firmly (though gently) guide clients through in order to help a fundamental shift in their mindset to occur.

Once they go through the doorway with my support there is no turning back, because once they have shone a huge light on their behaviour and patterns, and can see things from a different perspective, everything starts changing. Knowledge is power. Using proven techniques and methods, we plant these different beliefs and change takes place – sometimes slowly, sometimes quickly, but it's always about progress, not perfection. Some clients have stayed with their partners and their relationships have improved immensely because they have changed; some have moved on. Either way, they have the willingness to change, committed to our sessions and taken action, and I salute each and every one for doing so. It's brave and empowering.

Annie's observations

Can you recognise yourself now or at any time being deluded and making an excuse not to stand up and be heard or state your needs?

I have heard every 'yeah, but' under the sun and, quite frankly, they are all Doormat excuses. I only work with clients who quit being moaning minnies, stop talking about what is wrong and agree to do something about it. If anyone wants me to engage in their negativity and whinging, I say very quickly that there is no chance this will happen; I would prefer to clean a tube station with a toothbrush. I sit in the solution, not the problem. I am compassionate, for sure, but I use the tough-love approach and it works for clients who truly want to make changes. I am not interested in colluding in 'yeah, but'. After all, we have choices, every one of us, unless we have been made wards of court.

Now, Suzie wanted a commitment very much. She sees herself as supportive, fun, sexy, smart and giving, and she wants to share these qualities with a man in a commitment. She says she is real and after all what's not to love about a real woman? I think Suzie is all of those things and a fabulous woman, no question; however, unless she changes her mindset and behaviour she may not get the chance to utilise all these amazing qualities. I am not convinced that being real means staying a Doormat and not being honest. From the first date she directed all her energy and attention at Tim, proving what a wonderful person she was and what a catch she would be. She had no idea how uncomfortable this makes a man feel. She gets hooked in so easily to the wrong qualities in a man – his seductive technique, his charm, his cute butt, his humour. Even though she is an attractive, bright girl she loses all sight of what to expect from a man, and what she ought to give to a man.

I asked Suzie why she expected Tim to mind read. By this I meant that if she wanted a commitment and a family in the near future, how would he know unless she told him and they discussed it. I am not advocating anyone jumps on someone they have been dating for a few months and starts to discuss marriage, no way; but what's going on here? Suzie and Tim have been together nearly a year and they may be on the same page in many ways, but they are definitely in different books.

Tim is giving off several signals that he is not ready for a commitment. The first is that he is still married and not yet divorced – that's quite a big sign, I would say – and secondly he seems to be avoiding discussion at all costs about her flatmate getting married, and he's not coming to the flat any more. Another big sign. Lastly, he told her straight out that he doesn't want a commitment. How much clearer can someone be? Tim is being totally honest. However, Suzie can't hear it while she walks around town with her ear muffs on all the time. Therefore, while Tim is cooling off in many ways, Suzie is relentlessly pursuing him – and it's pushing him away even further.

Let's hear it for the boys

Time for a male perspective. One of my clients, Gary, is 36, bright, witty, attractive, straight-talking and very keen to make changes.

He came to see me as he was keen to resolve some issues around relationships. He wanted a relationship, but one that would go at its own pace and happen organically. He had been badly hurt before and not only was he treading carefully, but he was also very driven in his career and had a lot of goals he wanted to accomplish before settling down. He said that once he *did* settle down, he would put everything into it, as he wasn't a player and did want a commitment.

His last relationship with Steph had pushed him over the edge, as the same situation had arisen several times before and now something had snapped. He wanted to explore why he kept attracting the same type of woman. That's a whole different thing, but for the purposes of this chapter let's hear his experience of going out with a DoormaDiva (someone part Doormat, part Diva). Gary said:

'Steph and I had been together for about nine months and at first I was really flattered by all the affection and attention she lavished upon me. It was actually warming and comforting, then as time went by she got much more clingy and kept dropping subtle hints about moving in together. I felt under pressure. I had been honest from the start that I wanted to build my business and had a lot I wanted to achieve, so I wasn't ready to make a commitment. She was absolutely cool about that and said she was happy for us to enjoy each other's company and keep things relaxed.

'In fact I felt really irritated by her suggestions, as she clearly was ignoring what I had said, and the more she pursued it the more annoyed I became, then I switched off. The fact she was so keen made me suspicious, and I started thinking is it her body clock, or is it because her friends are starting to get serious with their partners, or is it because I am the most eligible guy in her life at this point, does she need structure or security, why is she constantly dropping hints about flats when she knows where I am with all of this? Is it a union she is after, one she feels I can provide and will take her to a different level? I started to feel objectified, as it was as though she had lost some of her pseudo-partners and wanted me to step in and fill that space, like I was the nearest, clearest option. I felt repelled and angry. I really did enjoy her company. She was bright, witty, generous, and she looked great and we had an amazing sex life – however, the more I stepped back, the more she chased. In the end I had to sit down with her and let her know I felt she was controlling the situation and trying to control me. I asked her to chill out and repeated what I had said in the beginning about not being ready for a commitment at this stage. She was not happy and in fact collapsed in front of me. First she was mildly shocked, then she got defensive, then angry and then it was like a "whatever" attitude. I couldn't believe it.

The other issue I struggled with, if I am totally honest, is that for a pretty girl she didn't have much confidence and needed constant compliments and reassurance. To begin with we had a laugh about it, but towards the end it turned me off. The truth is I felt at this point it was too late, and as much as I enjoyed what we had I was too angry and too uneasy that she wanted to lock me into a situation I didn't want, so I couldn't relax and be myself around her.'

Suzie has low self-esteem and a lack of self-confidence, and therefore needs external approval. This in turn results in her rational approach and intelligence disappearing. She totally dismisses the fact that she is enough with or without a man. It's so common for women to fall for charisma and not character, to fall for a guy's passionate kiss rather than his integrity or values. Suzie is needy for love and approval, so has never stopped and questioned for one minute if a particular man was reliable, grounded or even on the same page as her. To be perfectly honest, I believed that somewhere rooted in her subconscious was a false belief that she was the 12 or 13-year-old overweight midget who would never get any man to fancy her, so she now goes all out to prove she's awesome. Then she fawns all over any man who is half decent and gives her attention, and won't let go.

The paradox is that Suzie really wanted it to work with Tim but, like several of my clients, she kept a façade up and moulded herself to what she felt he wanted her to be, as she felt that if he saw the real her, he would lose interest. Firstly, this is dishonest and secondly, why not smile and say 'jog on'? After all, if someone won't accept you as you are, with all your flaws and assets, why on earth would you want to be with them? How can someone fall in love with you and get to know you if you don't show them the real you?

Suzie has such low self-esteem that she feels there is something inherently wrong with her, and she's right – what's wrong with her is that she doesn't feel good enough. If you don't drop the mask, how can you form intimacy? True intimacy takes time and we need to develop trust. I understand only too well what it's like to be spontaneous and it can be challenging restraining ourselves when it comes to attraction and passion.

When Suzie came to see me she clearly wasn't aware of her behaviour as she had been doing the same thing for so many years but, like so many others, she pointed the finger of blame at every other person and refused to look at herself. She was so focused on finding Mr Right but instead kept on finding Mr Right Now, and she claimed none of them wanted to commit. Suzie didn't realize that she was the one keeping commitment at a distance with her behaviour. I understood her only too well, having spent the best part of nearly a decade running around pleasing everyone else and putting their needs before my own. Do you know who I think I am? A no one, a Doormat, that's right; I am not important enough to warrant anyone respecting my needs and wants, or in fact opening my mouth and saying what would work for me… Oh no, it is you who is important – him, her and everyone else. My feelings don't count; no, sir, they are irrelevant. Your opinion and your point of view is far more important than my own. Why would anyone listen to me? The paradox here is that the most impressive people are the ones who don't try to impress. The more approval we look for the less we get. When we stop trying to impress others, others start to impress us.

Annie's solutions

Goals were set for Suzie:

- To grow and strengthen her courage muscles.
- To release her anger.
- To shift her negative emotions.
- To let go of old limiting beliefs.
- To raise confidence and self-esteem.
- To get motivated to find her voice and become assertive.

I work in a unique way. Over and over again, experience has taught me that one or even two methods used on a client are not enough for lasting change. I am a results-based coach so it's essential I achieve results; if anyone wants a quick fix, I suggest they go elsewhere. I am into lasting change, and therefore I blend a variety of techniques – and achieve amazing results.

Most coaches, although brilliant at what they do, offer one or two techniques and only a very few focus on confidence issues. I am one of the few coaches to do so and excel at this, as not only do I come from having had no confidence myself, but I walk my talk, and everything I suggest, I do myself. I truly believe that building core confidence, self-respect, self-esteem and accepting every part of ourselves is essential. Self-confidence and acceptance is the key. This is the base of everything. If I aim to tackle only the issue a client comes to me for, they may leave feeling inspired and motivated – and I can offer some excellent action points – but if we don't build a solid foundation, in time the floor will give way, the walls will crumble and we are back where we started. Healing must take place so we can peel away the layers of the onion and slowly unpeel the old limiting beliefs and hurts, release anger and negative thoughts. Then we can replace these with new empowering thoughts and feelings about oneself, new action points, and use new tools daily to bring about changes. If we don't have the confidence to make changes, nothing really changes.

I qualified in six techniques I felt passionate about and have had profound results with using them on myself. I've mentioned some of them before, and they are intuitive energy healing, coaching, motivational hypnotherapy, Theta healing, Louise Hay teachings, and Emotional Freedom Technique. I design a bespoke programme for each client, and if I feel it would be helpful, I also suggest acupuncture, bodywork, homeopathy, reflexology, nutrition or something along those lines from experts I know personally and highly respect. If someone has suffered trauma or needs to heal their past, I refer them to the amazing Noam Sagi of Kingyko Therapy, who is a very skilled body-centred psychotherapist and works in a unique way (his details are at the back of the book). If someone has untreated addictions,

I highly recommend 12-Step programmes, and you can find more information and details of those at the back of the book.

Let's look at Suzie's goals, and you'll see how this works.

Step 1 – to grow and strengthen her courage muscles

I used my highly attuned energy and intuitive skills to ask thought-provoking questions in order to bring about awareness, as I feel this is the prerequisite to change, as I've said. The first breakthrough was about school, which was a huge one for Suzie. I offered my observations (as above) and we processed this by email in between sessions. I suggested Suzie take some small steps each day to practise asking for what she wanted or saying things she had always been afraid to say. I asked her to make some lists and email them across to me and I would bookend her if she so wanted.

Bookending is great. I motivate and inspire a client to make a call or do something they dread, and then after they have made that call or done whatever it was, I support and champion what they have done. The reason for bookending is that many people bottle out of making a call or setting a boundary, but are less likely to do so if we have a bookend in place. Clients also often feel guilty or shameful when practising new behaviour, so speaking to me afterwards helps as I again reiterate how amazing they are to have taken this step.

So if Suzie wanted to get out of taking her small steps the likelihood was that she wouldn't if she had set a time for me to bookend. It also gave her courage to do it, and some support afterwards. It went like this. One action she emailed was that she wanted to ask her brother to stop saying something in front of her mum which she found totally disrespectful. She had never had the courage to say what she wanted to say for fear of upsetting him, plus she had always felt intimidated by him. She practised what she was going to say, ran it by me, then set a time to call me and call him straight after, and say what she had to say. This is not to criticise him or make him feel like a monster, but to say it firmly and assertively with loving care. Then she called me to discuss how she felt, and let it go.

Step 2 – To release her anger and shift her negative emotions

I suggested we had a session of Emotional Freedom Technique, the reason being that this amazing, non-invasive, cutting-edge technique brings about such huge results and clients can use it on themselves whenever they require. We needed to release the anger Suzie was holding onto so we could move forward.

Using EFT was very powerful for Suzie as while I tapped on her meridian points she focused on the bullying remarks at school and we shifted the negative emotions around it. She cried all the way through, then had a massive feeling of relief and a huge smile on her face, as she let go. No wonder EFT has an 82% success rate in the US and has been clinically proven to bring profound results for a variety of issues. Suzie used it daily between sessions whenever she felt anger, and very quickly the anger dissolved. I explained that anger is a mindset from which we operate in life. Some people constantly react and allow anger to rule the day. However, if anger is not vented at others or ourselves then there is nothing wrong, bad or shameful about feeling it. It passes through once we feel it and let go. We must not allow our emotions to bully us.

Remember, a thought is a thought and a thought can be changed. However, emotions and feelings are like wild animals; they are very patient, they wait and wait and wait for us to face them. If we run from them, they chase us. Someone once asked me 'How are you?' I said I was great. 'Cool,' he said. 'That'll pass.'

Some people are smart and channel anger into assertiveness. However, some use it in a destructive way and turn it on themselves as Suzie did, and I wanted her to stop beating herself up.

Step 3 – To let go of old limiting beliefs and raise confidence and self-esteem

Suzie was holding onto a lot of negative thoughts and limiting beliefs, low self-esteem and a lack of confidence which were not serving her. We needed to transform those beliefs into powerful ones which would help her move forward and help her build her courage muscles even more. I suggested hypnotherapy, so I could work on her subconscious and bypass her conscious mind with my positive affirmations. The cutting remarks bestowed upon her at school had affected her confidence without her being aware of it. I wrote out some simple affirmations and suggested she say them in front of the mirror. Research shows we each have around 50,000 thoughts a day and most of them are negative, so I suggested that Suzie saturated her mind with my basic positive statements, starting with five times a day and then repeated as many times as possible. The session was successful. Suzie was open, relaxed and absorbed all the positive data I fed her. How do I know? Firstly, she didn't want to get up and when she did she couldn't stop smiling.

These are her affirmations:

- I am bright, I have it right.
- I am more than enough.
- I am loving and lovable.
- I deserve the best of everything.

Step 4 – To get motivated to find her voice and become assertive

Suzie attended my workshops which are participatory in style, fun and packed full of practical tools around communication skills, body language and confidence tips to use daily. She also used EFT regularly on herself and I set some affirmations for her to use. We continued on with some more clinical hypnotherapy sessions and she started meditation classes which kept her calm and focused. She asked me to guide her around setting goals and as she blossomed and became assertive. It was a joy to witness.

Suzie has kindly written a few lines for *Doormat Nor Diva Be*. She says:

'I only intended to go see Annie for a couple of sessions to get my friend Jan off my back. However, if I am truthful it was a difficult time in my life and Annie helped me identify much more clearly the cause of my difficulties and work through them in a dynamic and effective way. I now feel totally at ease speaking my truth and asking for what I want. My confidence was on the floor when I started the coaching and it's incredible now to reflect back on how far I have come. I have quit part-time modelling, and am making huge changes in my life, with plans to move to the USA to study. I want to express my sincere gratitude.'

Reflection

Now, how about you? Where are you in your life right now? Are you a Doormat who wants to recover? Are you ready to grow your courage muscles? Are you willing to put the footwork in? Courage isn't always noisy; sometimes courage can be a quiet voice at the end of the day saying 'I will try again tomorrow'. It takes courage for you to decide to make changes and stick to them against the odds. It takes courage to change your opinion, mindset, habits and the path you walk. It takes courage to let go of old behaviour and patterns. It takes courage to find your own voice, go for what you want, stand up and be heard, be seen and feel worthy of having the best. Your willingness to take some risks is a measure of your willingness to live life to its fullest. Action is the cure for fear. Do you avoid challenges because of feeling fearful? Are you afraid to ask for what you want? What is the result you want? Imagine how you would feel if you got the result you wanted. What would you say? What would you do? What would it feel like?

• How many times have you pretended to be someone you are not?
• How many times have you been understanding of your partner about something when really you are not?
• How many times have you smiled and nodded in agreement with your partner when you don't really agree?
• How many times have you feigned interest in your partner's conversation on a topic in which you have no interest at all?

Question

What can you do today to make steps towards being courageous?

Actions

1. If you have avoided saying no to someone, say it now.
2. If you bend yourself around someone else's schedule and don't ask for what you want, say 'This is what I need from you, this is what I want'.
3. If you feel put upon, how about saying 'I love you, but I love me too'?
4. Write down two deal breakers and stick to them.
5. Get ready to go for it. Ask a friend to bookend you and offer to do the same for them.

Go and buy a gorgeous notebook and write a long letter to yourself. Forgive yourself for all the errors you have made and make a declaration to start – right now – making the changes you need to recover from Doormatism. Then let it go.

Read this chapter over and over, process it, answer the questions and take action. Start now. What are you waiting for? Can you afford not to?

4 Bye, Diva; hello, Gratitude Queen

If we are not grateful for what we have, why should the universe bring us more?

'I feel so angry I could scream,' Stacy said as she sat opposite me at our first session...

Let's meet Stacy

Stacy is 39, medium build, with long brown hair and hazel eyes. She wears little make-up, has a demure look and works as an executive secretary for a merchant bank in the City. Stacy owns a flat in Acton and has a fairly busy social life with close friends she has known for years, although she says many are focused on their partners and children now, and she is still very much a working girl and doesn't feel they have much in common any more. She loves the movies and open air concerts, and her hobbies include horse riding and painting – although she tells me she doesn't seem to have time to do either of those these days. She's an only child and was very close to her father who died of a sudden heart attack a few years ago, which had affected her badly, and says she has a fairly close relationship with her mum. She recently split with her partner of seven years, Sam.

First session

Stacy's pattern with Sam was that he used to stay over at her place a couple of times a week and they spent the weekends together, either at his home in Windsor or at Stacy's flat. Sam had joint custody of his sons, Mark and Sean, aged 11 and 13. Although Sam and his ex-wife had the boys alternate weekends, this sometimes changed. Stacy kept telling me how tolerant she was about Sam and his kids, but I wasn't convinced. She told me that she even allowed him to go on holiday a couple of times with the children alone. Interesting how she used the word 'allowed'.

Stacy told me:
'When Sam said he wanted to end the relationship, I was completely mortified and accused him of meeting someone else, which he denied and I do believe that to be true. However it's been five months and I feel devastated that he hasn't begged me to come back. I can't understand why he doesn't grasp that I am the best woman to have entered his life; I did tell him that at the time. The worst part is he won't explain why he wanted to split, and it's driving me potty; I keep asking if he will meet me and talk, but he says he doesn't want to as he doesn't want a drama. He said he hadn't been happy for a long time and felt suffocated. I really don't get that as we had space from each other a fair bit and we weren't in each other's pockets. I just feel so bloody annoyed as I have done so much for him.'

She went on to explain that her anger was directed at the fact that she felt he had ruined her life, and that her carefully constructed plans for the future were now in jeopardy.

'I met Sam when I was in Italy on a week's vacation with a girlfriend, and we immediately hit it off. He's a lawyer and was there on business. He wasn't my normal type at all – without meaning to sound unkind, I'd always been out with pretty suave guys who were flamboyant and good-looking and Sam is well presented and fairly tall, but not what I would describe as handsome particularly – but he struck me as being bright, gentle and generous.'

She paused and looked down at her shoes. 'We had some laughs and went for a meal a couple of times while in Rome, and nothing intimate took place. However we stayed in touch when we got back to the UK, and as he lived in Windsor and I lived in London, it was a bit of a pain getting together. He has two children, and had been divorced around five or six years when we met. He lived in Windsor to be near to his children. He seemed to have a fairly active social life and full-on work schedule, so for the first few months of dating we commuted between Windsor and London to meet up, even though I was insistent he made the effort most of the time to come to London; why should I travel to see him?

'For the first three months of us dating he wanted to keep our relationship a secret from his children. He felt he needed to get to know me first and be sure this was going somewhere before making the introductions, which I was fine about. It made things simpler for me in one way, but more complex in another as we couldn't get together when he was with them. When I met them it was awkward, but after two or three times going out together as a unit, it became fairly relaxed and we all got on well. We became more and more involved and he was honest in that he didn't want any more children. I was unsure at the time so that suited me, but it did become an issue towards the end of our relationship. After five years of dating I started feeling quite broody and refused to believe he wouldn't change his mind. In fact, I built up a fair bit of resentment about it.'

I asked Stacy to talk me through her anger. She said that all through the relationship she had been generous with her time and energy, and he had taken and taken and now he had left her. She explained how she'd invested so much in his life, telling him how he ought to bring up the kids, giving him advice on how to run his company and highlighting issues around his staff. She had also regularly pointed out that his ex-wife was bad news, and told him in no uncertain terms how his previous girlfriends had used him for his money. Didn't he see what an amazing catch she was? She wasn't after his money; she helped with the boys when they stayed over at his place; she was always on hand for advice; she organised holidays and ran their social calendar; she took charge of everything. So how could he leave her and why would he want to?

Annie's observations

Stacy had no idea as she sat there, taking Sam's inventory, how incredibly controlling she had been and how much she was deluding herself if she thought this was being kind and generous. In reality she was behaving as a true Diva, being completely arrogant in that she really believed she knew best. I suspected Sam was a Doormat, had attracted a Diva, and it had taken him several years to realise this (a delayed response). It's not so easy for anyone with low self-esteem and a lack of confidence to spot this behaviour immediately, as they rarely know any better. Once Sam was emotionally involved, I guess it became challenging for him to walk away from the relationship even though it was destructive. However, it was crystal clear to me that neither of them had discussed how they felt or had had any healthy communication throughout the relationship. They had just pushed their feelings under the carpet and carried on.

Being told all the time what to do is offensive, as it implies that we are not bright enough to work things out ourselves. That is a total insult and not a compliment. Unless Sam had employed Stacy to run his life personally and professionally, she had no business doing so. This is very multilayered, as there must have been benefits for Sam, as he'd tolerated being told what to do for seven years. Perhaps there was a part of him that liked being dominated, perhaps he'd been brought up by a domineering mother and knew no different – who knows?

There is a line I adore in *Sex and The City 1* where the girls are walking along Manhattan and discussing Carrie's next move, which one of the others feels is not going to work out for her. She offers unsolicited advice and Carrie turns to her and gently but firmly says 'Thanks so much for your concern. However, I am a smart girl and I will figure it out by myself'.

Stacy was not happy with me when I pointed out, gently but firmly too, that handing out unsolicited advice is patronising and not helpful, and that insisting other people do what we feel is right is a complete no-no. Most men tell me it makes them feel 'less than' and drives them away. She was indignant and defiant and became very defensive. She explained that she always gave advice, as why wouldn't she when she had so much wisdom? She still wasn't quite grasping it. She was so fixed on always being right and knowing what is best for everyone else, she just couldn't see that this was arrogant and egotistical.

Stacy also revealed that she felt resentful she wasn't number one in Sam's life, and I explained that is pretty much how it is when a guy has children – they take priority – and it was her choice to stay with him or not; let's face it, she knew from the start that he had family responsibilities and a commitment to his business.

She continued on, being damning about others and overly critical about Sam's ex-wife, some of the friends he had known for years and several of his staff. She felt that Sian, his ex-wife, was to blame for him being too scared to commit, that his friends all drank too much, that he was a workaholic – and on and on. She had an opinion on absolutely everything. She constantly pointed the finger of blame at everyone. She felt it was her responsibility and right to flag up everyone's shortcomings and, in a paradoxical way, she seemed to take much pleasure in doing so.

Stacy was playing out the following:

- PHR – proving herself right.
- COS – centred on self.
- WIHW – wanting it her way.
- GUA – giving unsolicited advice.
- NFF – not facing facts.

Let's look at these traits one by one.

PHR – proving herself right

Stacy spent the entire first session convincing me that she was right and Sam was wrong. I wondered who she was trying to convince. When people spend forever convincing others it is generally because they need to convince themselves, which stems from low self-esteem and insecurity. She had also spent most of her relationship telling Sam that he was wrong and then wondered why he left her. How many people are going to hang about with somebody who constantly criticises them? Why would anybody tolerate that? Well, unless their own confidence is at rock bottom and they have no self-esteem and therefore no faith in their own ability to make choices and decisions. It was not possible for Stacy and Sam to build and sustain a healthy balanced relationship while she was placing so many demands, expectations and judgments on him. It never seemed to occur to Stacy, even once, that she might have played a part in this break-up and when I suggested she consider the possibility, she looked genuinely shocked.

COS – centred on self

Stacy's agenda always revolved around herself: every move, every request, every tactic came back to her looking after her needs and wants without considering anyone else. She had no awareness of her own shortcomings because she was totally focussed on Sam and everyone else. At this point I knew in my heart I couldn't help Stacy in any way unless she grasped an awareness of her behaviour and was willing to make changes.

This, by the way, is not about shame or making Stacy wrong, it's about Stacy truly acknowledging first and foremost what her part was, taking responsibility for her behaviour and then having the humility to do something about it. If someone isn't doing something the way we want them to, or behaving in a way we want them to, and we feel resentful towards them, then quite simply we are being selfish. The world does not revolve around us.

WIHW – wanting it her way

Stacy was determined to have everything her way and, like all Divas, she reacted when she didn't get it. Now, to sulk when we don't get our own way at 5 years old is often expected and acceptable – but as an adult? That is *not* acceptable, at all. It is self-centred and unreasonable.

How can it be a relationship when one partner is calling all the shots and the other is dancing to their tune? That's an arrangement, not a relationship. For example, Stacy didn't like Sam to make any decisions about the children unless he consulted her. I understand completely that this can be tricky at times, as of course the children must come first and it can be difficult for the new partner not to feel last in line, but they are Sam's children and not Stacy's, and if she had an issue with Sam having children, why did she stay with him for so long? (And if Stacy wanted to bark orders, why didn't she buy a dog?)

GUA – giving unsolicited advice

This is a huge trait of every Diva. They love to be the queen or king pin and play the role of God. They attempt to tell you what is best for you and what you should and should not do and how you should feel, think, behave, dress, like, react – basically, they do not believe that you are capable of taking care of yourself. Now, don't get me wrong, many people initially love to be fixed as they don't have enough courage to listen to their own instincts, or are not confident enough to make their own decisions, or are often too lazy and want someone else to do all their thinking for them. In a nutshell, they have such low self-esteem that they believe everyone else knows what is best for them. These people are Doormats, who generally sniff out Divas (and vice versa), and for a while they can be a match made in heaven – until something changes. The Diva then becomes resentful when the Doormat rebuffs their advice – maybe they have become stronger or built their self-confidence and they suddenly realise that the Diva wants to fix them. How is this possible, when the Diva didn't break the Doormat in the first place?

I feel pretty certain this is what happened with Stacy and Sam. Often a Diva likes an adoring, submissive, self-denigrating partner. In fact, the Diva's sense of superiority depends on it. Stacy – like most Divas – acted unpredictably, irrationally and capriciously. A Diva's worst weapon in attempting to control others is their mouth. Stacy was charming, helpful, pleasing and witty, but she never accepted blame for anything that went wrong. However, she was always first in line to blame Sam, or his staff, or his ex-wife – anyone but herself. She expected to be the centre of attention at all costs and demanded that her every desire be fulfilled. She saw herself as being devoted to Sam's needs by offering him unsolicited advice on everything and wanting everything done the way she wanted it done. This is actually being a control freak.

NFF – not facing facts

Stacy wasn't facing facts. She was completely deluded; as far as she was concerned it was all Sam's fault. Everything would be so different if he did as she told him to, or he changed, or his staff were fired and replaced, or his ex-wife moved to Sydney, and on and on. Was she living in fantasy land? I would certainly say so. She was the one who needed to change. I am not saying Sam didn't have his faults – of course he did; we all do – but she was the one constantly trying to change everyone else and not considering that she might need to look at changing herself.

In order for me to even consider working with Stacy again I knew I had to ask her if she was willing to make a commitment to me, and to stop taking everyone else's inventory and look at her own. The facts were that what she was doing wasn't working, so was she ready to give up that old behaviour and take steps to move forward? When we initially spoke on the phone I had explained that I am a results coach, so I don't indulge in drama or negativity. If she wanted to sit in either, I was not the right coach for her and couldn't help.

Towards the end of our session, I asked Stacy to consider the following:

- If Sam wasn't giving her what she wanted, why did she stay with him for seven years and why did she want him back now?
- As she wasn't seeing, valuing or attending to her own needs and wants, how come she was getting upset at Sam? After all, he was treating her in the same way she was treating herself.
- If her acts of kindness and suggestions were from her heart, why did she feel so angry and resentful? We only feel angry or resentful

when we do things for others we don't genuinely want to do, but are deep-down seeking the love and approval which comes from the need to be needed.

Stacy burst out crying and sobbed for a good ten minutes. My heart went out to her. My own good girl/Diva role had robbed me of my life; playing the caretaker had cost me highly, as I had centred my entire life around my partners and neglected giving myself what I needed in the delusion that I would never be abandoned if I made myself indispensable. She had had that same 'ah ha' moment that I had experienced way back, the moment that changed things profoundly for me, so although I knew this was a painful realisation it was also a gift in that she could now start to take steps to change her life.

I suggested we swapped roles and I would play her and she could be Sam. I asked her to describe a few situations where she gave unsolicited advice. By the end of the role play she was incredibly uncomfortable and self-righteous and answered back on everything. She didn't like being treated like Sam; she said she was furious by the end at my arrogance and how dare I tell her what to do, and she also found it really offensive when I mocked her. This really made her sit up and listen to what I had to say.

Annie's observations

I felt Stacy was holding onto a lot of residual anger from her past. The anger that we hold onto always blocks us from becoming happy. It's not possible to be angry and happy at the same time, so I asked Stacy to have a think about if she wanted to sit in self-righteous self-pity or if she wanted to be happy and sit in joy. I felt intuitively that something had happened at school which had caused her some pain. She told me that one of her teachers had constantly humiliated her in front of everyone under the guise of helping her improve her studies. She said she had seen a therapist for about a year when she was in her early twenties as she had so much rage, and although this helped her understand why she was angry, it didn't take the anger away as she wasn't given any tools on how to do that, so nothing changed. She started to get where I was coming from as we had struck on a raw nerve. She burst through a massive bubble of delusion that day and, when she left, I knew instinctively we would be doing some great work together.

In the next session I explained that there would be no quick fixes as change requires patience, commitment and practice. It was clear to me that we had to look at her resentments, which were huge, around helping Sam and his family and his staff for seven years and not helping herself. Acting as a martyr was her coping habit and she had an unconscious need to get what she was giving. Stacy had a driving need to run the show and call the shots; she was being as highly critical of herself as she was of others as she couldn't stand any form of imperfection. Divas are skilled manipulators and rehearsed debaters. Winning is an obsession for them. The more you give, the more they take.

Annie's solutions

Goals were set for Stacy:

• To help her release her anger.
• To help her let go of old limiting beliefs.
• To help her practise super self-care.
• To learn interpersonal communication skills.
• To explain the importance of having gratitude in her attitude.

Step 1 – to help her release her anger

There are so many ways to work around this. I knew that – as Stacy had understood her resentments were causing her mood swings and knee-jerk reactions – it would be helpful to offer her practical tools to use every day when these challenges arose.

I offered her some EFT to help with the anger and showed her how to do it at home, whenever she felt the anger creeping in. I explained this was incredible with diffusing surface anger, but to get rid of old, buried anger we needed to do some healing work, and so we set up some hypnotherapy sessions and Theta healing. These sessions were incredibly powerful and she let go by crying continually for about twenty minutes. The tears reside underneath the anger, so this was great progress. She said she felt like a balloon which had been popped, as she had always struggled with crying and so felt it was a huge release for her. Another vital tool was to use assertive techniques she had picked up in my workshops (see Chapter 5), as resentments are not able to build up when we are behaving assertively because we are respecting ourselves and saying how we feel at that moment in time, something which is empowering. I also suggested she consider kick-boxing as this is an amazing way of releasing anger. She could get as angry as she wanted with the bag she was kicking or the person she was boxing with, imagine it was the person she was really angry with and go for it.

Step 2 – to help her let go of old limiting beliefs

Again, there are many ways to work with this. Limiting beliefs are affirmations we tell ourselves over and over and we therefore end up believing them to be true. Habits are the function of the subconscious mind. If we repeat a thought over and over again, we can choose that thought to be negative or positive; it's entirely up to us. No matter what our limiting beliefs have been, no matter how stuck we feel, we can turn things around. We need to hold the intention of the person we want to be, and find our authenticity. If we have a neon sign on our forehead, we must be sure we know what it says to describe us. The only thing stopping happiness and harmonised relationships is our own behaviour, our thoughts and mental imagery.

Visualisation is the key, and it's used by many high achievers, either naturally or through discipline. By this stage in the book, it's no good any of us saying 'I know all this'. Are we actually living it? If not, then we do not know all of this. Knowing something and taking action on it are two entirely different things.

The mind does not know the difference between fantasy and reality so our thoughts and feelings make something real. However, this does not mean we can visualise and expect things to change without taking action; no way. Quantum physics tells us we hold our world together with our attention, so I suggested to Stacy that she focus her attention on what she wanted, not on what she didn't have or what had gone wrong. I suggested she tell herself it was time to let go if she was fearful of change; that what she was doing was not bringing her the life she wanted, so she needed to tune into another station and stop giving her fears airtime and energy.

I took her through a guided meditation and visualisation and we worked on her rapid breathing, slowing it down to bring her back into alignment and therefore helping her stay in the moment and not trip onto 'tomorrow or next weekend', instead to be here now. She was so busy waiting for the big moment that she hadn't a clue that this was it: this was the big moment, right here, right now.

When she became relaxed, I asked her to picture herself on a plasma screen and visualise a scene with Sam where she reacted to something he said or gave him orders. I asked her to really feel within and tune in to her high-pitched voice and notice her breathing rate rapidly rising, study Sam's body language and response, notice what she is wearing, how she moves her hands, smell any smells in the room, to study every single thing around her as if she is actually there, and make it as real as possible. I asked her to say firmly 'this behaviour is passing away now' over and over and over again. I then asked her to visualise the whole scene again and this time see herself as a calm, serene and powerful woman listening to Sam in an empowering way, pausing for a moment before responding and breathing slowly and gently, but speaking assertively in a rational, even tone. I suggested she do it each night to get familiar with her new way of behaving and get comfortable with it.

The affirmations I suggested were:

- I am calm and confident.
- Every word is valued and heard.
- I learn to listen and listen to learn.
- I respect others and they respect me.

Step 3 – to help her practise super self-care

I think Stacy thought I was a bit crazy suggesting this step and was quite hesitant at first. I explained it might not sound like it was worth the effort but assured her it would make a massive difference. Firstly, it raises confidence and self-esteem; secondly, when you focus on yourself, you are far less likely to be focusing on everyone else – as Stacy tended to do.

So I suggested she start to build a relationship with herself and she agreed to meditate for five minutes a day in order to still her mind, get centred, learn how to control her thoughts, start listening to her intuition and train herself to be focused.

There is no right or wrong way to do this, but let me tell you it will make a difference to your day, especially if you do it consistently. Lie on your bed or the floor or sit in a chair. Focus on your breath and let yourself feel relaxed. If your mind races to the emails you didn't send yesterday or the fact that it's raining and you left your umbrella somewhere or the things you need to buy for supper tonight, don't worry. Gently bring yourself back to the present moment. Count slowly from one to ten and then back; this will help you stay focused.

I suggested to Stacy that as she lived with herself all the time, it was a pity that she didn't have a relationship with herself.

I asked Stacy to be mindful of what she put into her body to preserve her energy, and to ensure she drank one to two litres of water daily. Starting the day with hot water with a slice of lemon and root ginger is something I learnt way back in my modelling days; it kick-starts you in the morning and cleans your skin, and even though lemons are acidic, the body processes them in a way that leaves an alkaline residue. I suggested she also ensured she had good levels of protein at every meal. My experience and research suggests this keeps blood-sugar level, and you are therefore less likely to get cravings and mood swings; I am not a nutritionist, but have studied nutrition for over twenty years and know what works for me and the clients I work with. Exercise is also vital, as an inflexible body equals an inflexible mind. I suggested Stacy keep a mindful eye on who she hung out with. Toxic, negative people would drain her emotionally, so if she hung out with the blamer, the complainer, the drainer, the shamer and the gossip she was wasting her money coming to me. How could she move forward and stay in a positive mindset if everyone around her was trying to pull her back to how she used to be so they didn't have to look at their own stuff?

I also suggested that she got to bed at a reasonable time, ensured she had regular dental and medical check-ups, kept her clothes organised and her home free of clutter. She said she didn't have a problem with keeping her clothes and home tidy and organised, but didn't have time to do the rest of the things I suggested. I pointed out that this wasn't surprising as she was too busy playing the martyr and running around after everyone else.

You see, when we do estimable things, our self-esteem rises enormously and our inner confidence soars. When we practise super self-care we start attracting people to us who treat us with respect and value us as we value ourselves. When we look good, we feel good; when we have a self-care structure it becomes a habit and that's a great routine to get into. Stacy said it would be a challenge to start focusing on herself, but she was willing to give it a go.

I gave her a technique to apply when she felt the urge to dictate and offer unsolicited advice. It may sound simple and it is, but it is also very effective. When someone reveals their issues, often they look to someone to listen rather than leap in and fix them, so when Stacy had the urge to leap, I strongly suggested that she check with her breathing. If it was slow and calm and there was no charge, then it would be fine – once the other person had finished speaking – to go ahead and ask if they would like some feedback or suggestions about how to overcome the issue. If, however, her breathing was racing and she had a charge and a compulsion to leap in, she was to say nothing and actively listen instead. If she wanted to, after the other person had finished speaking, she could offer a hug. When we experience calm, deep, slow breaths and actively listen to someone's challenges, we are coming from a place of tolerance, love and compassion. Sure, if it feels right, we can offer some feedback; otherwise the best thing we can do is genuinely demonstrate love and compassion by giving the other person a hug. The fast-paced breath and charge comes when our ego needs to jump in and be heard, to flag up what the other person is doing wrong, to illustrate that we are right and to act in a self-righteous manner, not really having any interest in what the other person is saying or feeling any empathy for what they are feeling. It's all centred around meeting our own needs and proving how smart we are. Simply put, we are playing God. For Stacy, implementing all this would have a double whammy effect. It would improve her relationships radically and also reduce her anxiety and stress enormously, and ensure she would not deplete her energy tanks.

I suggested choosing some of the following: acupuncture, reflexology, herbal wraps, cranial-sacral osteopathy, shiatsu, aromatherapy, facials, pedicures, body scrubs, manicures, hot stone massage, energy healing, reiki, tai chi, yoga, Pilates, Indian head massage – whatever grabbed her fancy. Things like these are no longer considered a luxury; in this day and age they are necessary. We all need to call time out and have time to reflect, relax and replenish.

I went on to suggest Stacy bought an air filter to purify the air in her bedroom, and tried deep breathing exercises, inspirational reading, fun movies and anything that made her feel good. If she got off track it was no big deal; she just needed to gently get back on.

Step 4 – to learn interpersonal communication skills

I will touch on this very briefly here, as there's some more detail in Chapter 5. I explained to Stacy that there was a difference between a demand and a request, and having strong, healthy communication skills meant being able to state our needs and wants clearly and honestly while also respecting the other person's wants and needs. It would be essential that Stacy started with an honest self-diagnosis, and recognised the long-standing destructive patterns which had caused her endless issues in her life.

Step 5 – to explain the importance of having gratitude in her attitude

Stacy, like all Divas, had the attitude that life owed her a living and took everything for granted. But why would the universe bring us more when we are not grateful for what we have already? Stacy (like myself) had a history of severe depression. It is not possible to be grateful and be depressed; neither is it possible to be depressed and feel grateful. I decided many years ago to follow what Oprah Winfrey had said worked magically for her – to create a gratitude journal, and even if I felt low I had to force myself to write five things I was grateful for in it. When you are depressed that can be a huge task to undertake. As I had been in that dark place, like Oprah, I was at a stage where I was willing to try anything – and I found this changed everything. It has been one of the most incredible tools I have ever used. Accepting and respecting ourselves, walking through fears by taking action and being grateful are three tools which I find work wonders. It's not what you do once or twice that makes any impact; it's being consistent that determines the results in your life.

When we have gratitude we raise our vibrations so we attract in more. Danni Minogue said this on her TV show: 'I have found by being happy and grateful I have attracted in amazing things.' She is so right.

Stacy says:
'Since working with Annie I realise I have spent my life being a queen reactor. I moaned, I groaned, I complained and I blamed everyone. I really get now that I was full of fear and needed to be right, rather than happy. I may have been mature in years, but I was very immature in many ways, hence reacting like a child when I didn't get my own way and having tantrums and chucking my toys out of my pram. I took everyone's remarks personally and made everything into a drama. My head was so busy. I should have said to other people, "apologies if my head is making so much noise, but I am organising my life as well as yours, so it's pretty full-on".

'Annie has helped me realise that I am only responsible for my own actions and choices and I can only change myself, no one else. It feels pretty liberating, actually, not judging everyone else and allowing them to say and do whatever they want without jumping in like a raging banshee.

'When Annie said to me not to lie to myself about my behaviour, and that it was time to tell myself the truth and become proactive rather than reactive, that really pulled my heartstrings. I cried as I realised gossip, criticism, negative energy and being so reactive had knocked me off balance all of my life. I had expended so much time and energy fighting battles, controlling everything and everybody, and it was a waste of time and completely pointless.

'I can't believe the difference it has made practising self-care; I wish I'd done this years ago. I feel so much more confident inside and way better about my body. Eating healthily and having a structure has meant that not only has my self-esteem risen but so has my energy, and by reducing stress and anxiety through regular meditation I am more focused and much calmer. It's amazing how many people have commented on how different I seem, but they can't put their finger on exactly what the difference is. However, I can – it's everything; my attitude has changed so much, everything around me is also changing, and although at first it felt scary, it's now feeling exciting.

'From the moment I made a commitment to myself to rise above the need to be heard and be right and start listening to myself instead, everything started shifting in my world. I can't explain, but I felt it strongly as for so many years I'd needed validation from others. Now I'm totally not bothered about what anyone thinks of me and I don't need to strut about like a Diva. I want to invest my valuable energy and time into my visions, dreams and goals and building a relationship with Stacy.'

Reflection

Stacy really grasped that she had made life much harder for herself by repeating old patterns that were no longer working. She felt a lot of sadness around losing her relationship with Sam, and yet felt by identifying her patterns around men she could start making changes, and that gave her hope. After processing everything we discussed and discovering more about herself and her core values, she realised that Sam wasn't the one for her.

This all may have been a blessing in disguise. He had made it clear he didn't want any more children; he had also made it clear that he didn't want to move to London. Stacy knew in her heart that she wanted someone who lived in London, as she was an ardent townie and, while she didn't have any issue being involved with someone with children, she did want one of her own and time was of the essence. She also really knew that Sam hadn't been ready to commit fully and used his responsibilities around the children and having a full-on job as excuses for not taking things any further. She had denied all of this to herself for so long. She kept thinking that if she pointed out constantly how fabulous she was and kept trying show him where he was going wrong and how he ought to run his life, he would see he couldn't do without her. This backfired, as it so often does; it pushed him away and, on a subconscious level, he may have contracted and closed down, and that could be why he has even refused to discuss things. Something snapped inside him before they split which propelled him to walk away.

Stacy realises now that she has pushed many men away without realising her sabotaging behaviour. She says she was so wrapped up in herself and her own needs that she hadn't really given a thought as to why her relationships went wrong. Therefore she pointed the finger of blame at all her exes, and then berated herself for picking men who let her walk all over them and then walked out on her.

Question

Do you believe you are worthy of super self-care?

Action

Fake it till you make it by taking one action a day out of Stacy's super self-care plan – see Step 3 above – and just do it!

(If money is an issue with an option you might like to try – such as Indian head massage or Pilates – find a local college or training school where they often offer them at ridiculously low rates.)

5 Bye, silence; hello, voice – where have you been?

Remember: those who matter don't mind, and those who mind don't matter

Now that you understand how Diva and Doormat behaviour affects your life and causes you and others discomfort and pain, can you see how your life is (and has been) limited by your fears?

Here's the thing. Life is like a game of cards; the hand that is dealt you represents determinism, but the way you play it is free will.

I have faced some of my greatest fears: the death of family members, a partner's suicide, the painful ending of relationships, redundancy with no redundancy payment; significant health issues, severe depression, a chronic eating disorder, betrayal from close friends, family members and partners. Throughout all of this, I have received my greatest gifts: courage, gratitude, tolerance and compassion for myself and others, inner strength, humility, grace, self-confidence and acceptance.

Building voice muscles

Facing and walking through our fears builds confidence and emotional strength. It's vital to develop tools in order to stand up for ourselves and no longer avoid anything through fear. When we do that, all that happens is that the issue becomes larger and larger – and it always waits for us, so running from fears is futile. If we do, our confidence gets crushed and our self-esteem dips to zero.

- Martha said she got upset when Matt left crap in her car after he'd borrowed it; he always promised to clean up but never does, and yet she found she couldn't say anything.
- Tracy wanted to ask Steve why he had condoms in his bag after being away with the boys for a week but was nervous of any confrontation, so she said nothing.
- Helena wanted to ask Mark to stop complaining to her about his work and look for another job, but her voice muscles contracted and she remained silent.
- Tess was tired of Stuart always borrowing money, but couldn't find the courage to say anything.
- Anita was really uneasy with the fact that Neil kept flirting with her friends but said nothing.
- Janine got so angry with Rob when he used her expensive moisturiser that she screamed at him.
- Katy got upset when Tim was late for a date and scolds him, like a mother does when angry with a child.
- Marina wouldn't speak to Peter if he forgot to bring home her favourite ice cream when he did the weekly shop.
- Karen withdrew sex from Trevor when he didn't do as she suggested.
- Sarah wouldn't cook for Martin if he came home late after seeing his mates on a Saturday afternoon.
- Teresa hid Tom's beers if he forgot to bring back her clothes from the cleaners.

It's amazing how a Doormat's natural reaction is to say nothing when upset, while a Diva's natural reaction is to shame, punish or scream. None of these reactions are good and, if I may say so, they are also extremely childlike. Not the actions of a powerful twenty-first-century woman.

Many of us are so needy for approval and being liked by everyone that we automatically say yes and don't consider the consequences, or we say nothing and don't consider the consequences. These are habits we have carried around since we were children. Many of us become martyrs, and like my client Stacy end up full of resentments. Not everyone is a people-pleaser, striving to win approval; some say yes because they dread confrontation of any kind.

Read below and see if any of the following resonate with you?

- When faced with conflict, you feel sick in your stomach and panicky about the need to stand up for yourself or feel charged up ready for a drama.
- When someone confronts you, instead of speaking your truth, you find yourself agreeing and apologising or screaming and being unreasonable.
- When upset over a situation, you find you have a committee in your head replaying over and over what you could have said, or you have a knee-jerk reaction and lash out, only to regret it an hour later.
- Instead of facing a confrontation, you light up a cigarette, pour yourself a glass of wine, eat a packet of biscuits, obsessively clean your house, go shopping and buy things you don't need or pick up the phone and 'fear junkie' (moaning, complaining, being full of fear, gossiping) to a friend.

If any of these apply to you, it could indicate that you have low self-esteem and no inner confidence. However, fear of confrontation can often stem from witnessing parents screaming and arguing over everyday issues when growing up and/or them walking away after an argument with us or someone else. If your parents overreacted with rage or shame around some things, the chances are pretty high that it will impact on how you respond to conflict as an adult.

Because of this, most Doormats react by closing down and saying nothing, and most Divas react by becoming aggressive. I always refer clients to a therapist if they have experienced violence or trauma of any kind when growing up as I feel deeper work is required. I strongly recommend combining talking therapy with bodywork to shift fear and trauma, as unresolved emotional issues are stored at a cellular level. Therefore, as helpful as it is to have talking therapy, fear and trauma need to be shifted from the body – where we store memories and retain fear – in order for us to experience lasting change.

Once we start becoming assertive, know what our values are, own our power and set and maintain boundaries, it becomes a natural way of life, believe me. People react so differently towards someone who does this that I can assure you that you would never want to go back to being Ms Doormat or Ms Diva again.

Get acquainted with your values

Have you ever taken the time to discover what is truly important to you? It's such a great exercise as it helps you form a strong relationship with yourself and understand who you are. When you accomplish this, you can form a strong relationship with someone else.

Read the list below and follow your intuition and put a tick by the words that leap off the page. There are no rights or wrongs, it's as it is. We each have our own set of values and they prescribe our attitude and character. They determine which aspects are important to us. They reveal our tastes, our way of life, our social, political and personal interactions. Some of our values can be 'superficial', transitory or fit with the situation in which we find ourselves. Other values are fixed and stay with us throughout our life. These are our 'core values'. Values come from a range of sources; parents, schools, friends and colleagues can all have an influence upon our values. Conflicting and unfixed values can often confuse us as teens. I find it incredible that I have asked so many clients, colleagues and friends what their values are and they don't have a clue. If we don't know what our values or core values are, we are disconnected from ourselves and this can bring lack of fulfilment, discontent and unhappiness.

Many women I know are trying to live a life according to their partner's values, rather than living a life according to their own core values. This means their partner's values are being met and theirs are not, which can lead to resentments, frustration, low self-worth and a lack of confidence, and can even cause a couple to split.

Do this exercise two or three times. Remember, read the list and put a tick beside the words that leap out at you. Whatever you do, please don't start analysing as that would be paralysing; just jump in and go for it. This is not about what you 'should' choose, it's about what you 'want' to choose, through how you feel.

Take some time to process your first list. Does anything surprise or concern you? Then do it again and this time ask yourself 'do my relationships help fulfil my personal values?'

Sensitivity	Attract	Thoughtful	Honesty	Directive
Passion	Connect	Encourage	Health	Design
Compassion	Accepting	Motivate	Influence	Tolerant
Accomplishment	Sensual	Educate	Trustworthy	Respond
Adventurous	Leader	Independent	Responsible	Invent
Acquire	Triumph	Transform	Consistent	Security
Family	Thrill	Gratitude	Sincere	Freedom
Directive	Nurturing	Inspire	Authenticity	Excellence
Learn	Touch	Fun	Artistic	Unique
Support	Perfect	Entertain	Contribute	Risk
Willing	Inform	Commit	Courage	Speculate
Humour	Vulnerable	Romance	Dedicated	Wealth
Experiment	Sincere	Peace	Open mind	Patient
Dedicated	Plan	Integrity	Observe	Learn
Success	Power	Relationship	Growth	Spontaneous

Remember that core values often alter over time. As you unpeel more layers of yourself, and get to know who you really are on a deep level, you may even find that if you decide to come back and do this again you pick different ones.

Come on, get assertive

Once we are acquainted with our values and core values, it means we will find it far easier to become assertive as we will want to live a life according to those core values. Of all the workshops I hold, the one on this topic is always the most popular. I wish it could be introduced into the educational system somehow; no one teaches us at school how to stand up for ourselves, so how are we supposed to know this stuff? This is where we start taking back our power. We teach people how to treat us. Tell me, how do you want to be treated?

We must stand up for what we want, state our needs clearly and calmly and remember that assertion is not synonymous with aggression. Assertive techniques ought to be used only to produce results that benefit both parties. We are equal to everyone else, not better or worse, so always communicate from a position of equality duality.

Let's meet Tricia

Tricia is 35 and works in IT. When she came to see me she had been going out with Paul (who works in the same organisation) for around eighteen months. He was one of her bosses but based on another floor, and she had a line manager she answered to daily. Paul liked to remind her that he was one of the bosses and when it was coffee time, and they were outside having a cigarette, or lunch time – when they occasionally headed off to the local pub with some of the team from work – he would belittle her in front of colleagues. Everyone found it amusing that she was the butt of his jokes, so she always laughed along with them and let it go over her head, and he would often wink at her or say 'She's my princess, she knows I'm only joking' whenever she looked a little hurt or went quiet. Tricia had been tolerating this for a year. The first six months of dating was heaven, she said, as Paul was the king of charm and seduction and she fell for him big time. He was handsome, generous, witty and bright and she'd been single for a long time, so she felt blown away by him immediately.

I gave Tricia five tips for her to put into action.

1. *Take a deep breath*
On average, 38% of our message comes from our tone of voice, so when being assertive it is crucial we take that into consideration. Breathing relaxes the muscles around the jaw, which tend to tighten and affect the way we sound. Talking quickly tends to go with dominant and aggressive behaviour, so bear that in mind. If we speak in a high-pitched voice we are reverting to childhood, and will instantly lose the other person's respect. Breathing deeply and speaking slowly will counteract many of the anxious reactions that can be detected in our voice.

2. *Practise, prepare, plan*
We need to get really clear and be fully rehearsed on what we are going to say and how to respond to possible reactions from the other person.

3. *Talk to yourself*
Never underestimate the power of the spoken word, whether to ourselves or another person; what we say to ourselves feeds our beliefs and in turn our perception of the world. The brain hears this mental chatter and believes it to be fact and will adjust behaviour accordingly. Telling ourselves we are confident, capable and strong is powerful.

4. *Mind your language*
Remember that if we get triggered, so can other people. Language is crucial if we want to defuse rather than escalate a situation. Aggressive language is insulting, bossy and argumentative. Being patronising is also offensive. Telling people to calm down is being passive-aggressive. Saying 'I understand, but…' can often start a row. Many aggressive statements start with 'you should…', 'you must…' or 'you can't…' Change these to 'I appreciate how you feel, but this is how I feel…' When we use the word 'I' it shows we are owning our own thoughts and feelings, rather than putting them onto the other person. It is also very empowering and builds cooperation and understanding.

5. *Body language*

The body communicates a huge percentage of our message. If we avoid eye contact, we are being passive. If we clench our fists or point our fingers, we are being aggressive. To be assertive, it's essential to limit hand movements to soft, flowing gestures that support our words. Look the other person in the eye. We must be really focused with our message – voice, body and hands.

Key pointers

Divas, do not talk over the other person or allow them to talk over you; do not shame them or insist on being right. This is not a competition. Doormats, stop apologising. It's crucial for a Diva not to attack someone's character or sulk, and for a Doormat not to take everything that is said so personally.

If you are a Doormat or a Diva, you need to ensure you are not patronising, defensive, reactive or self-righteous. The most effective way to communicate is to be direct and rational and if someone is manipulative or intimidating, they may try to wear you down until you give in, so be prepared for that and stay focused. Listen carefully to what they have to say, see their point of view, have respect for them, and be gentle yet firm.

Being assertive means determining when to speak up and when not to. You cannot be assertive if you are charged up, so you need to discharge all your emotions in order to communicate effectively. Change your language, hold your ground, and remember that no one has the right to violate anyone else. Smile, nod and encourage the other person by saying 'uh huh' and summarise their comments periodically. Active listening is a model for respect and understanding in order to gain information and perspective. There is nothing to be gained by attacking or putting someone down. If you are candid, open and honest and assert your feelings and opinions you are respecting the other person – and yourself. Always treat another person in the way you want to be treated.

Another pointer is the interest-based relationship (IBR) approach. It means always remaining constructive, even when under pressure. Label the behaviour, never the person. Good interpersonal communication skills require a high level of self-awareness, and so by understanding our personal style we will do so much better. By learning to be a good listener we will improve productivity and our ability to influence and negotiate. Doormats and Divas need to resolve conflict; Divas must respect other people's interests and Doormats must respect their own. Both often need to mend damaged relationships.

Tricia tried everything I suggested, but Paul kept giving her slippery responses and was non-committal about changing his behaviour. Tricia was now starting to back down and tell me that maybe she was being a drama queen and that he didn't really mean it; after all, he had a wicked sense of humour. I therefore suggested she either tolerate it and let her confidence reach rock bottom, or she tried something else and built her confidence up – so she agreed to try something else. There were three possibilities.

1. *Broken record*
I suggested Tricia kept repeating herself and refused to be deflected by his slippery responses until she finally got an outcome which was mutually acceptable

2. *Fogging*
Tricia could train herself to remain calm when Paul put her down and then fog him. By this I meant responding with 'yeah, I agree' or 'you are probably right,' or 'your point is…'. You see, when we fog someone we rob them of their destructive powers. Although this may come across as being fake in a way, it's very powerful as we are sending a message out that we don't allow anybody to disempower or intimidate us. We are stating that we own our power and do not give it away to anyone. This way they don't get to act out on us – and many Divas get a kick out of making others react.

3. *Following DESC scripting*

- D – say what seems to be happening.
- E – express how it is making you feel.
- S – say what you want to happen.
- C – explain the consequences.

When Paul put her down, Tricia need only go through each step succinctly and firmly. The consequence could be either 'If this happens again we are done' or 'We would get on lots better if you took a different approach, or understood where I was coming from with this.'

Tricia says:
'When I first spoke to Annie about this I felt really fired up and determined to take action and confront Paul, even though I was terrified. I was so scared he would leave me, and then Annie pointed out that if he did this, wouldn't I feel pleased he had revealed his true colours as a bully who wanted to put me down and squash me so he could feel empowered? I thought about that for a few days and I decided that, yes, I would take the risk and walk through my fears, but to be honest I hadn't prepared myself as Annie suggested so it all went pear-shaped and I lost my footing. I stuttered and wobbled and then went back to Annie and said maybe I was being too sensitive and perhaps I needed to just learn to shrug it off. She asked me whether I wanted to build my confidence or shrink it, and I said I wanted to build it, so I agreed to try one of the other techniques. I therefore decided to opt for the fogging and Annie and I role-played so I felt much more comfortable and prepared when I finally plucked up courage to tackle Paul.

'Much to my amazement it worked like magic. He poked fun at me about something while we were with friends and I remember Annie saying her favourite one was "if you spot it, you got it". That tumbled out of my mouth and Paul looked totally aghast, and I so wanted to laugh. However he said something at the end of the evening and I said "And your point is?" His face was a picture and, do you know, he hasn't made any remarks to me since that night, it's pretty incredible. I know he still does this with colleagues at work as I have overheard people's conversations and caught him at it a few times, but he hasn't tried it with me. Guess he feels there is no point, as he won't get the reaction he used to as I'm not playing that game any more. It's amazing and has lifted my confidence so much in other areas of my life. This is a tool I shall carry around every day. I'm telling you it really works to use these techniques, and so I'm really pleased I didn't contract as I used to and cave in to his inappropriate behaviour.'

Fences make good neighbours, right?

What do I mean by that? Well, do you have boundaries? If not, do you know where you end and other people begin? If your relationship is filled with more of what you don't want and not enough of what you do want, it's definitely time to start setting boundaries.

Having no boundaries means we don't know what is inappropriate and what is appropriate behaviour and therefore don't know what to do, ask or say. Having damaged boundaries means we cannot figure out who is a friend or foe and therefore look for people to take charge of us (Doormat) or we take charge of them instead (Diva).

There are different sorts of boundaries:

- Walled boundaries – being trapped and imprisoned; no one can come in and no one can get out.
- Physical boundaries – having the right to determine who, when, where and how we will be physical with someone else.
- Sexual boundaries – having the right to determine who, when, where and how we will be sexual with someone else.
- Emotional boundaries – having the right to feel what we feel when, where and how we chose to.
- Intellectual boundaries – having the right to think what we want to think.
- Spiritual boundaries – having the right to believe what we want to believe.

Many Divas disrespect Doormats' boundaries. They physically hit, shove or push their partners when they get angry or don't get their own way. They use sarcasm, ridicule, call them names, go deadly silent on them, become spiteful. Many Divas who are in relationships dominate their partners sexually and emotionally, and often use overt touching in unacceptable ways or make smutty jokes in inappropriate situations.

Setting and maintaining our own boundaries is a way of honouring other people's boundaries, and can be confusing and challenging within relationships. Having boundaries is a good way to exhibit self-respect.

Unhealthy boundaries

Here are some examples of damaged boundaries in action:

- Falling in love with someone we don't know.
- Allowing someone to be sexually abusive with us.
- Letting our partner define us.
- Going against personal values to please him/her.
- Letting someone else direct our life.
- Being preoccupied with someone else and neglecting ourselves.
- Revealing everything to someone new within the first few weeks.
- Not noticing when someone is invading our boundaries.
- Believing others can anticipate our needs.
- Allowing someone to take as much as they can from us.
- Not noticing when someone displays inappropriate boundaries.
- Acting on the first sexual impulse.
- Letting someone else describe our reality.
- Saying yes when we mean no.
- Allowing someone to manipulate us.

Healthy boundaries

Positive boundaries:

- Define who we are.
- Demonstrate to others how to treat us.

- Help us know what thoughts, feelings and behaviours are appropriate to have towards other people in a relationship.
- Let us feel safe enough to remove walls of defence.
- Enable us to feel confident enough to be who we are.
- Let us feel confident enough to determine what is acceptable behaviour from others.
- Help us to feel empowered enough to not allow anyone else to manipulate us.
- Mean that we feel empowered enough to have self-discipline and strength of character.
- Let us feel confident enough to say yes when we mean yes and no when we mean no, and do so with ease.
- Define what we are and are not responsible for.
- Delineate how much time and energy we have to give.
- Separate our thoughts, feelings, wants, desires and needs from those of others.

We filter our experiences through our cognitive mind and our feelings. Through the use of our boundaries we determine which words and actions we will accept and which we find unacceptable.

What are your boundaries?

....

....

Where do you draw the line?

....

....

How do you react when someone sets boundaries with you?

....

....

Let's meet Tania

Tania had no boundaries when we started working together.

Tania says:
'I came to see Annie at a time where I felt exhausted with my relationship as Danny and I had met just four months before, but already patterns were appearing that had caused me grief in old relationships, so I wanted to break them. I didn't have a clue what boundaries were when Annie spoke about them, but what I can tell you is that I allowed Danny to run the show, that's for sure. I felt tearful, tired, anxious, and responsible all the time for doing what was good for him. I carried around all his feelings and if he sulked when I didn't do what he wanted I felt so much shame and guilt that I always caved in, then ended up apologising to him. The thing is, I've done that with every man but something snapped inside this time and I thought I am really done with this, really done with this.

'For example, Danny would call and start speaking and I would say "Babe, I am with a friend and we are out shopping on the way to meet some other friends," and he would get all stroppy that I wasn't able or willing to drop everything and spend an hour on the phone to him. I used to get so angry inside as I would never expect anyone else to drop everything when I call them, not him and not my girlfriends. I would suggest we speak like later, and his response would be punishing like "forget it" or "your friends are clearly more important to you" or "I'm not around for the next few days."

He is 40 and yet he behaved like a 12 year old. My point is, I always did what he wanted to keep the peace, and I see now that I enabled his behaviour. If he hung up (which he often did when I wasn't there 24/7) my whole day and evening would be ruined. Every time I felt shame and felt really bad, every time, and I had enough. So my friend Michelle suggested I see Annie – queen of boundaries, she called her, not that I knew what that meant. I am 38 and I don't want to be in another relationship where I am the one who is being controlled. I want to be equal and I want to give and take and I don't want these dramas any more. What I was clear about was that I was the one attracting these men, so I knew I had to take some action and change the pattern. Annie made me laugh, when I asked why I kept attracting the wrong type of men, she said it wasn't so much why I attracted them, it was more why I gave them my mobile…

'Annie and I started play-acting the situation so I could get used to speaking up for myself in a way that would be effective. At first, to be honest, it was so uncomfortable and I realised what a complete pushover I had been for so long, so I really beat up on myself. However, after going to several of Annie's workshops I started realising I was far from the only one who did what I had done for so long and that was very comforting. We paired up and shared this "nice girl" behaviour and suddenly the shame I felt disappeared as I was able to laugh with someone else about how crazily co-dependent I must be and how there was no way it was going to continue. Annie explained to us that often when we move out of the "nice girl" role we have a lot of suppressed anger and can be too aggressive and rigid when setting boundaries, as we are scared of being used and hurt again, but this is not the way to go, so we need to find a balance in being boundaried and yet flexible. I found that really challenging and it was honestly a matter of practising. When I first started approaching Danny using my new tools, he was not happy and I remembered Annie saying that if a guy doesn't respect our boundaries it's unlikely he will stick around. That means it's unlikely he would have stuck around, even if I wasn't putting down boundaries, as the guy who is a stayer and not a player will not be put off by me placing boundaries. With that in mind, I decided it will go whatever way it goes and he will reveal his true colours, so it's a win–win situation. That gave me more confidence than ever to stand up for myself as I am not at the stage or age in life where I can be bothered to waste time and energy on someone who is not into me for the long haul.

'The guideline I was given was to keep the topic I was addressing in the present and not wonder off into the past (which I can be very good at doing). I was to wait until Danny responded before giving my reaction and to comment on an observable behaviour, not a character analysis. I found it hard to not respond to him complaining with a cross complaint of my own – in fact, when I practised it with Annie, she had said it could be challenging at first, and if I remembered to do so it would help to take three deep breaths. I did this silently and it really helped.

'I really want to focus on finding the right partner for me, not the almost right partner, so when Danny split with me I felt pretty relieved, to be honest. He showed his true colours by not wanting to hang around when I started laying down boundaries. His explanation was that this was becoming more trouble than it was worth, charming! I now believe I am worth the trouble, so good riddance to Danny. I have photocopied the bill of rights Annie gave me and carry it around in my bag, so I don't slip back into old habits.'

This is what I gave Tania.

OUR BILL OF RIGHTS
- I have the right to express what I want and I need.
- I have the right to set my own priorities and boundaries.
- I have the right to be treated with respect at all times.
- I have the right to express how I feel.
- I have the right to make mistakes.
- I have the right to change my mind at any time without feeling guilty.
- I have the right to express my uncertainty or confusion.
- I have the right to be treated as an intelligent and capable person.
- I have the right to decline responsibility for everyone else's problems.
- I have the right to express my opinions, thoughts and beliefs.
- I have the right to choose my own values and follow them.
- I have the right to say yes or no.
- I have the right to be who I am.
- I have the right to walk away if anyone shouts at me or talks down to me.
- I have the right to be valued and heard.
- I have the right to say it as it is.

- I have the right to own my power.
- I have the right to strut my stuff!
- I have the right to decide what is best for me.
- I have the right to like what I like without justifying, defending or explaining.

Reflection

Let's get one thing clear here: the era of long-suffering, self-deprecating women in relationships is over. No longer was Tania convinced that Danny was the best she could do. She got really clear in our next few sessions and workshops about who her ideal man was and decided she would pass up on every Mr OK and hold out for Mr Great. Why? Quite simply, her confidence had risen radically and she was realising she was worth it. She wanted a commitment so she decided to practise her boundaries, use her voice and go on dates, but keep herself available for someone who valued her and respected her for having her boundaries. I suggested she didn't focus so much on changing her behaviour but more on shining the light on it, so that her old behaviour would start to feel uncomfortable and would then start to change organically. We can only change when our beliefs change, and by setting boundaries and raising her self-esteem, Tania started to believe in herself.

Question

Who do you need to set a boundary with?

Action

When will you set it?

6 Will the real you please stand up?

Wouldn't you rather be yourself than be a poor imitation of someone else?

Many people spend their lives rehearsing to be someone else for years, then look baffled when I ask them directly 'Do you know who you are?' So please read these thought-provoking questions several times over.

- What stops you from being you?
- What games do you play?
- What is it you hope to win?
- Are you disguising your true self to fit in?
- Are you trying to be what everyone expects you to be?
- Are you becoming someone you are not?
- Are you trying on the identities of people you admire and walking about wearing them?
- Is your true identity buried under layers of other people's beliefs?

No matter what your situation is, being yourself will take time, focus and a willingness to set aside any preconceived ideas about who you feel you ought to be, how you feel you ought to act and how you should feel. You will need to focus on what you want, what you feel, how you think you ought to behave and who you feel you truly are. You only have one companion throughout life and that's you, so why not make friends with your closest companion?

Your core lies underneath your false self, your mask, your public persona, and there is nothing more amazing than going on a journey of self-discovery, getting to know yourself. How can anybody be intimate with another person until they have forged an intimate relationship with themselves? If you don't know what you feel, like or want, how can you share any of those feelings with anyone else?

Do you know what you...
think?
judge?
feel?
value?
honour?
want?
love?
hate?
fear?
mean?
desire?
hope for?
respect?
enjoy?
believe in?
feel passionate about?
feel committed to?

Make a note of each one of these and list your answers next to them. This could be very revealing as these are some of the things that will define you as an individual, make you stand out in the crowd from everyone else. Although your answers to many of the above will change constantly, don't you think it would be a good idea to know what they are? (This is a more advanced exercise following on from the value system in the previous chapter.)

I hear a lot of my clients say 'I am afraid to show people my real self; if I do, they may not like me any more.' How sad. Why do we think we are so awful, unlovable, unlikeable? Our deep fears and insecurity will keep us imprisoned. There is nothing wrong with us aside from our negative thoughts, and we can change those.

After all, I am sure none of us would feel proud about living a lie or being a phoney, but when we are steeped in fear we don't want to risk being honest and so we stay hidden behind a mask and play games.

In each of us is a variety of ego states, and an acculturated self and a deliberated self. The culture in which we live is one of the sources of our programming and sets us up to react to certain situations in certain ways. When we constantly oblige others by people-pleasing, we stay in patterns that have been determined by our past, and our acculturated self becomes an actor. Clients who come to me say they get so much awareness and insight about themselves that they start becoming more comfortable with themselves and so, organically, what happens is the deliberated self – which acts out of conviction – takes over and they become more authentic.

Playing games

When we play games, they aren't fun: they are fake and they are old, repetitive reactions to life situations programmed for us somewhere in the past. Sadly most people are playing to win, so these games can be dangerous. However, it is really good to shine a bright light on our old programming and become honest with ourselves about how we are behaving. Remember, (as I keep saying) awareness is the prerequisite for change.

The games are shields which we carry around while we are in battle. We may have used them up until now as survival tools to protect ourselves from being rejected, used, hurt, neglected, abandoned. So this pattern sets up an ongoing situation in which we use our survival tools to win the battle and that makes us feel empowered and inflates the ego. It's all fake, so what's the point?

These games defeat self-knowledge and wreck all possibilities of healthy, strong, honest communications, and so we end up paying a high price for victory. If we were to rid ourselves of our fears and insecurity and low self-esteem, and get in touch with who we were and how we feel and really tap and tune into that, so much in life would change.

If we don't speak up and be who we really are, we will act out. Feelings are like steam gathering inside a boiling kettle. Suppressed but gathering strength, they can blow the human lid off just as the steam inside the kettle will blow the lid off the kettle. Suppressed emotions can also come out in other ways such as headaches, skin rashes, allergies, asthma, common colds, aching backs and limbs, fatigue and constant sickness, clenching of fists, slamming doors, rising blood pressure, temper tantrums, violence, grinding teeth, tears… Let's face it, they have to go somewhere. Don't ever think that our feelings will disappear if we ignore them. They are very patient and will always wait for us.

Here's the thing. We never bury our true feelings; they always remain alive in our subconscious minds and cause us hurt and sadness. As a clinical hypnotherapist I witness this all the time.

We may fear that others may not think highly of us, or may reject us, or punish us in some way for our emotional candour, or withdraw love and affection. If any of this happens because we are being ourselves, then I would seriously put a question mark over these people we call our true friends. True friends accept us as we are – end of story. However, remember that if we're in a relationship with someone and not disclosing our truth, we are being dishonest and fraudulent. If we build a relationship on anything less than openness and honesty we are building it on sand and it will never stand the test of time.

Get real

We need to get to know ourselves by knowing what we feel, think, believe… If we communicate these things freely and openly we will find a noticeable growth in our own sense of identity along with a deeper and more authentic knowledge of the other person. We can only understand as much of ourselves as we have been willing to express to someone else. Big changes will start taking place for us, *big* changes.

For example, let's say you are competitive, and allow the emotions under your spirit of competition to surface so you can inflate your ego. You may find that it was only your sense of inferiority, your lack of belief in yourself that propelled you into competition. Have you considered that?

When these emotions are allowed to illuminate our inner selves, they can tell us things we never knew about ourselves. This kind of self-knowledge is what brings about profound changes.

Here's another example. You may be feeling really destructive, and if you allow this to rise up and stay inside, it will show itself as self-punishment. (Most 'depression' is self-punishment, by the way, or deep sadness/anger turned inwards.) If you stay with this despair it could highlight the fact that you have guilt and shame within. When you can recognise these emotions as negative and self-destructive, it is then within your power to move these emotions to a new reaction: from self-pity or self-punishment to self-love; from anger and irritation to empathy, and from despair to hope.

It isn't up to me to prove this to you. Why not try it and see what happens? Don't take my word on anything, just do it and that will be enough proof that this stuff works.

Incidentally, lots of people get away with being rude and offensive and saying 'Sorry, but that's the way I am.' This is a delusion. It's a great excuse to use when people don't want to take responsibility for themselves – it's a cop out.

Once we get attuned to our emotions and feelings, and are aware of what we need and want, we will feel empowered and aligned and others will feel safe with us, as they'll know that what they see is what they get. It's a great place to be. Once we trust ourselves, others trust us; the dynamics will change within us and in our relationships, personal and professional.

Our senses, emotions, feelings, and thoughts as individuals need to be integrated. Most interpersonal conflicts arise from emotional stresses (anger, jealousy, frustration, etc.), and most interpersonal encounters are achieved through some sort of emotional communication (e.g. empathy, tenderness, feelings of affection and attraction). In other words, our emotions and how we deal with them will either make or break us.

If we feel angry over differences of opinions, we can ask our anger how it got there and where it came from. If we feel shame or guilt, ask them how they got there and where they have come from. We may not uncover the whole core, but we will get a glimpse of an inferiority complex, low self-esteem or low confidence or something else that we may not have been aware of before, or perhaps hadn't admitted to ourselves before.

If anger or irritation arises while we are speaking to someone, it's best we stop the conversation as we need to discharge all emotions and be rational and calm. Often we defend our dishonesty on the grounds that it may hurt others, and so we compromise our integrity to people-please. Some of us rationalise our phoniness into nobility, and settle for a superficial relationship with others. If we are at a dinner party and are served something which we can't stand, then why would we force it down just to keep the host happy? Isn't that a bit odd ?

The paradox is that many of us are unwilling and reluctant to tell others who we are and yet we have a deep desire to be understood. Here's the thing: we will always walk around feeling alone inside and misunderstood if we are not being ourselves with others. Everyone has secret dreams and secret pasts, broken dreams, secret shames, and that's OK. I am not suggesting we reveal everything as there is a huge difference between being revealing and honesty.

No one has ever had our exact thoughts, our exact experiences, our exact feelings, so why would we be ashamed? This means we are unique and, in my book, means we are precious. Why wouldn't we celebrate that? Anyone who has a good self-image truly accepts who they are, and is at ease with themselves. Believe me, people always want to be around those who have self-confidence and self-acceptance, as both those traits are highly attractive.

To thine own self be true

When we divulge our true self and the person we are doing this with holds our hands or hugs us, reassuring us with gentle compassion in their voice and has complete empathy and offers support or understanding, it is the most amazing experience. When we are taken seriously, understood, supported and really listened to, it feels simply wonderful.

It is only through this kind of sharing that we will come to know who we are. Introspection of itself is helpless. It's only when we share true acceptance and intimacy with someone else that we can experience being our true self. True friendship and truly deep relationships are a great adventure because there is a continuous deeper discovery of ourselves and the other person as we continue to share new and deeper layers of ourselves. It opens up our minds, fills us with new awareness, deepens our feelings and feels great.

We always pay a price for pretending to be someone we are not, as we will never be able to keep up the pretence. What happens is that our authentic self gets hidden behind the mask, and so we remain duplicitous. That's such a pity. We deny others the pleasure of seeing the real, authentic us, but why? To make matters even worse, we eventually lose track of who we really are. We often begin to take on values and beliefs of others and change who we are to slot in with others.

When we are not standing in our truth we become so bent on fitting in and being accepted. Often when we are behaving in this way we don't even realise it as it's 'happening' subconsciously.

Stop rehearsing to be someone else

Once we lose ourselves in the process by trying to be someone we are not, we may get nervous that someone will expose us for who we really are – and that's a really uncomfortable place to be. Being ourselves may feel uncomfortable at first. However, everyone is flawed and nobody is perfect, so we need to accept all of ourselves and run with it; it's more than enough. When we accept and embrace our imperfections they lose a lot of power and we feel empowered.

It's essential that we tell the truth about ourselves and by this I mean:

• What we like and don't like.
• What we are looking for in a relationship.
• How we feel at any given time.
• Our tastes, beliefs and values.

Although we always run the risk of turning some people off by telling them who we really are, the rewards far outweigh the negatives. Why not risk being who we are, as it's the most important risk we will ever take? It is extremely refreshing to hear people tell the truth about themselves and many respect them hugely for doing so – after all, it hasn't done Simon Cowell any harm. Telling the truth about our strengths and weaknesses lets people know that we are not superficial and trying to impress them, and that we have depth and honesty and do not have any shame around our more shadowy parts. It is incredibly powerful to be honest and be who we are. People are always drawn to real people.

If others don't know the real us, they are being deceived. Eventually this backfires on us as we can't keep the pretence up all our life. However, if we are with people who are slippery and dishonest, it would be foolish to open ourselves up as this invites them to take advantage of our vulnerabilities. We must never, ever, allow any situation to develop where we introduce ourselves as the 'emotionally wounded soul' and view the other person as 'above us'. We can still be honest without telling it all. We need to aim for relationships that are equal, not ones where we are seen as the weak, neurotic or needy person.

Self-acceptance is the key

By telling the truth and being ourselves, we begin to attract those who genuinely like and appreciate us for being the real us. That means all the people who are impressed by a false façade will disappear from our life. By being ourselves, we will raise our self-esteem in a profound way and our confidence will rocket. We will accept and appreciate who we truly are and will not attract those who are looking for somebody they can manipulate and control.

We will become more self-assured and stronger within. One of the best ways to complete the individualisation process is to put ourselves out in the world, to make a statement, take some action that defines us and separates us from everyone else. Basically, exposing our true self creates a stronger self.

Once we set a precedent by being honest about ourselves, it makes it a lot easier to start asking for our needs and wants to be met, and to speak up when we don't like something. Being ourselves will involve owning our anger, pain, fear, guilt and shame we may have suppressed for years. It means finally being able to speak out loud. It means discovering a way to communicate our beliefs, deepest feelings and thoughts with ease, and acceptance of who we are.

- Tracy felt it was rude to let her boyfriend's mother know she didn't like meat, so she now hides it in a napkin when they go there for lunch and hasn't said anything to her boyfriend. How does she know that his mother only cooks the meat because she thinks Tracy loves it, and would prefer to cook tofu as meat gives her indigestion? Tracy has assumed she can read his mother's thoughts.
- Mary didn't like to tell her dad she couldn't stand opera, so he keeps booking tickets for the opera when she comes to London. How does that make for an honest and loving relationship, allowing him to spend all that money on tickets when she can't stand it?
- Teresa didn't want to let her partner know she wanted a child, as he had such a bad split with his ex and horrendous problems with custody of their son. She feels he might therefore be nervous about committing to having another child, but hasn't approached the subject and feels upset as she is nearly 40, and children are definitely on her agenda.
- Sarah didn't feel it was kind if she said to her husband that she wasn't ready to move to France and start their own business. She loves the

job she is in and her friends and family are really important, but she doesn't want to upset him so she's going along with it.

• Charmaine didn't want to upset her sister by telling her she couldn't call her at work, and now she's always getting told off by her supervisor for taking personal calls.

• Marina couldn't stand long walks and country pubs, but didn't want to upset Michael; after all, they had only been dating for six months.

• Judy couldn't tolerate loud rock music but said nothing; Mark loves it, so she goes along to concerts with him to keep him happy.

• Jenni doesn't like Thai food but Tim adores it, so she feels she ought to just go along to keep the peace and say nothing.

• Hannah was irritated that Steve always wanted to go on sports holidays when she preferred to lie on a beach, but he pays so she feels she must oblige.

• Martha didn't agree with any of her flatmate's views on politics, but pretend to agree as she didn't want to upset her.

Can you see where all these clients were pretending to be someone they were not? Most of them have spent so long faking it that it's become a habit.

Get a pad and pen and be really quiet for a moment. Take some deep breaths and complete the following statements:

I feel angry when...

I feel safe when...

I feel embarrassed when..

I feel guilty when...

I feel shame when..

At the moment the thing I feel most ashamed of is.........................

At the moment the thing I feel most angry with myself for is..........

....

These thought-provoking questions help you connect more deeply to your emotions, help you discover who you are, help you work out your deepest desires and listen to your inner voice. And all of these will help to empower you.

You must not judge yourself for slipping and sliding during this transition period; it's always progress. Remember each attempt brings you that much closer to finding inner strength, self-belief, self-esteem and confidence.

No matter which path you follow, the most important thing is discovering the authentic self instead of focusing all your energy on people-pleasing. In reality, it's what you don't express that can get you into trouble. The more you pretend to be someone else and repress your true self, the more likely things will burst apart when you don't expect it.

Get your pen and pad again and let's get going on some more insights. Answer these questions:

- Do you always try to fill in silences during conversations?
- What are the aspects of yourself you deny?

Then carry on:

- List all the parts of yourself you feel shame and guilt around.
- Now list all your assets.
- Write down an example of a time when you felt resentment with yourself for not being honest in a situation with someone.
- Write down an example of a time when you were indecisive in order to avoid responsibility and keep someone else happy.
- Where do you seek recognition?

Take action

It's only through being vigorously honest that we will get to know ourselves. As we get to discover ourselves more deeply and reveal new and deeper layers of ourselves, we open up our mind, widen our horizons, fill ourselves with heightened awareness and deepen our feelings. Being real involves daily change and growth. We must continually express who we are as we are continually evolving.

An ego defence mechanism is called 'projection'. Many of us tend to disown parts of ourselves and 'project' them onto others. Trying to rid ourselves of our own shortcomings by attributing them to someone else doesn't work. It's very common to dislike in others what we dislike in ourselves. The paradox is that we don't recognise these things in ourselves, and often people strongly condemn traits in others that they cannot admit to in themselves. The stronger or the more exaggerated the dislike of anything or any quality is manifested, the more it should be suspected of being projection.

The most common form of ego defence is 'rationalisation'. As a technique for self-justification, it is hard to beat. We find some reason for our action which justifies it. Often there are two reasons for everything we do: the alleged good reason and the real reason. Rationalisation is not only self-deceit but eventually corrupts all sense of integrity. We rationalise our failures; we find justification for our actions; we reconcile our ideals and our deeds; we make our emotional preferences our rational conclusions.

As with all ego mechanisms, there is always something which we cannot or do not want to admit in ourselves, something that would make us feel better if we could believe it. Rationalisation is the bridge which makes our wishes the facts. It is the use of intelligence to deny the truth. It makes us dishonest with ourselves and we certainly can't be honest with anyone else. It consequently sabotages all authenticity and disintegrates our personality.

Not being ourselves and being insincere is an interior state of mind, and is a psychological impossibility. We can't tell ourselves that we do and don't believe something at the same time. It's a two-way street. If we are honest with others about triumphs and tragedies, agonies and ecstasies, it will help us face our own, and we will become an integral person. I greatly admire people who are vigorously honest. That takes self-confidence.

When we always need to be right it is because we are insecure and our self-esteem is threatened. It basically demonstrates that we're not confident and have deep, and subconscious, doubts about ourselves and our opinions.

Ask yourself this: do I need to be right, and if so, why?

What role do you play?

The Fool

Sally always behaves like a clown, always messing around and trying to make people laugh. It's because she is desperately seeking attention and sadly believes that playing the fool is the only way she can gain approval and recognition. On a deeper level, it's frequently also because she identifies with her act and tries to evade reality by not taking anything seriously. She tells me she often doesn't know how to handle herself in a serious situation or how to react around sadness. I feel that's why she behaves so irresponsibly and childishly. The mask she wears is her clown's mask, one to prevent others knowing who she truly is and how she really feels. It's easier for Sally to laugh and deflect grim realities and make out she is an actress on stage rather than face issues full-on and reveal her true self.

The Competitor

Mary told me she'd become obsessed with competition and wanted to win at any cost, so she made everything in life a 'win–lose' situation. She didn't discuss, she debated. The triumphs she sought were often at the expense of others. Her insecurity caused her to question her worth, and she consistently tried to prove it in competition and rivalry. Her need for recognition intensifies the drive to constantly 'get ahead'. She said she felt hostility towards anyone she thought was standing in her way or surpassing her. She often got frustrated as she couldn't always prove her superiority. Basically, the problem was that Mary couldn't distinguish between being herself – Mary – and what she accomplishes.

The Peacemaker

Trina wanted to keep the peace at any price. She felt the need to conform as she couldn't risk others not approving of her. People could think Trina was cool as she went along with things, but at what price to her sanity and peace of mind? I asked Trina why she thought it would help to suppress her emotions. She explained she wanted praise from others. I asked her why, but she couldn't give me an answer.

The Big Shot

Alison tended to drop names and be 'me-centred'. Both traits come from low self-esteem and zero confidence. She went around trying to dominate others, constantly telling people what they ought to be doing. Again, this is low self-esteem and lack of confidence. Alison constantly needed to control and to show off by letting everyone know who she had met, who she knew and what she had achieved, as that made her feel worthy.

The Gossip

Nadia always gossiped, and by doing so she chose to elevate her own self-esteem by undermining the esteem of others. After all, it is much easier to tear down others than lift yourself up by your own achievements. Superiority and inferiority being relative terms, diminishing other people raised her own status. Nadia gossiped and put others down so she wouldn't have to feel so badly about her own misdeeds. However, I pointed out that it was neither her right nor her responsibility to flag up anyone else's shortcomings.

Quit playing games

Judy admitted she had low self-esteem and zero inner confidence and so I wasn't surprised when she admitted that she behaved in an aggressive way at times and liked to have the upper hand. She revealed that she was nervous about making decisions as she felt she would lose respect from others if her decision turned out to be wrong. She had a really short fuse and never spoke openly about anything. She so needed to be needed and lent out her wisdom, rather then encouraging others to use their own strength and develop their intuition. She is a caretaker and comes from a place of not feeling enough being who she is, and feels she is only worthy of being friends with others if she helps them. In fact, the reality is that what Judy is doing is dominating others emotionally.

Judy resented her friends as she used up so much energy offering unsolicited advice and ended up accomplishing very little. Her resentment has become an emotional habit. Her feelings are not caused by others; remember, nobody can upset us unless we allow them to. Judy has choices about everything and her feelings are caused by her own emotional responses and reactions. When she reacts and becomes resentful, she becomes a reactor, not an actor, and is left with no self-respect.

If any of you do things like this, isn't it time to quit playing these games? Get out that pad and pen again.

Write down an example of a situation where you say nothing or nervously talk too much without getting to the point.

....

....

....

....

....

....

Now write down how you would rather behave, what you would like to say. If I was standing by you saying you could be yourself, what would be different? What would you say? How would you appear?

....

....

....

....

....

....

Now write down what's stopping you. What are you afraid of? What is the worst thing that can happen?

....

....

....

....

....

....

Affirmations

Now let's create some simple yet effective positive self-talk or affirmations that you can use and keep repeating every time you have doubts. Remember that everything you focus on expands, and so why not focus on the positive rather than the negative? If you think any of these negative thoughts, delete, delete, delete and say the opposite every single time:

Negative –I can't be myself.
Positive – I am proud of myself.

Negative –I am scared he/she won't like me.
Positive – What people think of me is none of my business.

Negative – No one listens to me.
Positive – My every word is valued and heard.

Negative – I want to be perfect.
Positive – I am perfectly imperfect.

Negative – I am not good enough.
Positive – I am amazing.

Negative – I cannot be myself.
Positive – People love me more when I am myself.

Negative – I can't say no.
Positive – I say no with confidence and ease.

Negative – I need other people's approval.
Positive – I approve of myself.

Negative – If I take care of my own needs, people will walk away from me.
Positive – I am only responsible for myself.

Negative – It scares me to speak my truth.
Positive – I feel comfortable saying it as it is.

Negative – I will get hurt if I express my truth.
Positive – People respect me for speaking my truth.

Negative – Everyone judges me.
Positive – Everyone accepts me as I am.

Negative – I can't be honest with people I love.
Positive – The people I love appreciate and respect me for being honest.

Negative – Nobody ever asks my opinion.
Positive – My opinions are valued.

Reflection

I cannot emphasise enough how being honest about your dislikes and likes, and being a hundred per cent honest, will make such a dramatic difference to your life. It means that you don't have to put up with activities and behaviour from others that you don't like any longer. How amazing is that?

Perhaps telling the truth about your preferences may disappoint someone and they may wish you agreed with them but it won't usually put them off totally. If it does, then they only wanted you in their life to be able to use you – in which case you are better off without them.

By stating up front that you don't like X, Y or Z, other people won't expect you to go along with their preferences, and you won't agree to, even if they do. Being yourself is so powerful and makes it possible for you to find people who have similar interests, beliefs and values. Just imagine how exciting it will be to express your opinions and preferences about everything from politics, religion, art and food to your favourite hobby, and find that the people you surround yourself with have similar preferences and opinions; even if they don't, they will love your confidence in speaking your mind. What a waste of time and energy it is to pretend to be someone you are not, and be dishonest about what you like and don't like to fit in with others.

Question

What have you learn about yourself from this chapter?

Action

A very useful exercise is to describe yourself as you would in a personal ad. Include as many likes and dislikes you can think of. Start writing...

Now read your ad back and carefully determine just how honest you have been. If you haven't been completely honest about who you are, then go back and rewrite your ad and get a hundred per cent honest.

Make sure you have included the preferences that are most important to you, and that describe the kind of people you really want in your life.

Remember that you do not have to put up with anything that offends, irritates or is insulting out of politeness. You don't have to go into depth about how you feel around your childhood or the row you had with your best friend to anyone. However, you do need to honour yourself and be proud of who you are as this encourages others to be honest – then you are being real and this is where magic happens.

You are amazing – so get out there, my friend, and *be yourself.*

7 Where do I go from here?

Whatever we have discussed in this book, I think you will agree that the root of all of our problems are low confidence, low self-esteem, and obsessions with needing everyone else to accept us, validate us and approve of us. This behaviour is what causes us not to be authentic, and sadly most people in the world are running around the globe being fake and dishonest. How crazy is that?

The addiction to be loved and accepted by everyone permeates all areas of our lives and our relationships with ourselves and others. The deep need to people-please keeps us bound in relationships that are not healthy and not satisfying. If we continue to run around seeking approval on the basis of what others think of us, we destroy our essence and crush all our confidence, crumble our self-esteem and chip away at any self-worth or self-belief we may possess. Doormats (who are so invested in keeping others happy at the cost of their own happiness) and Divas (who insist on controlling everyone and everything) will be constantly dissatisfied and unhappy deep down. It is so damaging to our self-esteem to be at the mercy of other people's opinions and we reinforce the negative patterns we already have by being so. It's essential that each one of us learns to approve of ourselves and accept that we are more than enough, exactly as we are. We all waste so much energy and time trying to get other people's approval when we could be channelling that energy elsewhere. It's always good to be open to feedback, and always interesting to ask others their opinion of what we are doing, but we then need to honour ourselves by believing that we are smart enough to listen and trust our own intuition, and do what's best for us whether or not the other person agrees, approves or supports our decision.

Many people like to dump their insecurities, fears and issues on us, but firstly we do not need to allow that, and secondly we don't have to agree with them. Give up plugging into their hang-ups, beliefs and self-righteous attitudes about how we ought to behave, think and feel. Sure, everyone is entitled to a point of view, a belief, an opinion, but that all belongs to them so don't put it in your own bag and carry it around. Give it back.

You are the final authority on your life. No church, no partner, no teacher, no guru, no organisation, no friend, no system knows more about what you feel or think or believe or need or want than you do.

It's always empowering to work with a coach or a mentor, someone who has walked the path before us and can help guide us when we are unsure, but the minute they become an idol is the minute when we lose sight of the message. I have a client who is in recovery from alcoholism and she says in AA's 12-Step programme, they say 'Never listen to anyone in AA, listen to the AA in them'. As the 12 Steps state: 'it's principles before personalities'. That is amazingly powerful. As I've said, I don't have all the answers – far from it – but some clients and friends have unrealistic expectations that I can give them the solution to all their problems. That's far from reality; I have blind-spots, prejudices, and my own lessons to learn and path to follow. I respect the mentors I work with and am grateful they are in my life, but I do not worship them or necessarily agree with everything they say. It's the message and not the messenger that counts. It's essential that we learn to lose our expectations of others and allow everyone to be who they are – and allow us to be who we are.

Who are you? What do you want? Are you happy? Get clear on who you are, what you want and write it all down and respect it. Doormats: do not let others impose or inflict their views on you; Divas: give up inflicting and imposing your views on others. Who has the right to say the way we choose to live our life or the partner we choose to date or marry is wrong for us? I completely accept myself, my views, my thoughts, my beliefs, my actions, my choices and I have many close friends who support me, and I learn from them and listen to them when they offer feedback, but ultimately Annie Ashdown is Annie Ashdown's best friend. I am the captain of my own ship, and that's for sure. I don't go around thinking I know it all, but I do make my own decisions and trust they are the best ones for me. I will not allow anyone to manipulate me by pushing my vulnerable hot-spot buttons as that is them wanting to control me, not support me. After all, I have no control over anyone else's life, any more than they do over mine. I cannot stress enough how unacceptable it is for Divas to put words in Doormats' mouths and try to programme them to react in the way they want them to.

It is totally out of line for Divas to behave in an irritated or angry, hostile manner when Doormats don't act or react as the Divas think they should. Divas: you need to grasp that you do not get to run the show, however much you feel you are entitled to do so. Doormats: you need to give up craving for a Diva's attention and approval to the point of inflating your own virtues, and let go of those insecure fears about not feeling good enough that haunt you. That inveterate people-pleaser and approval-seeker within you will keep you wrapped in fear, zero confidence and low self-esteem. Sure, there will always be people who are offended by limits but they are the ones who are trying to control and manipulate us. Some may even say we are being selfish by saying no, but the bottom line is this:

Our responsibility is to ourselves, not everyone else, and where would we get the time to take responsibility for others and why do we feel that's our role, anyway? Why do you think passengers on airlines are told to put lifejackets on themselves first? We get to decide what's best for us, and if we don't grasp this, perhaps we ought to consider why we have such a deep-rooted need to be needed and such a deep-rooted need to be known as 'the nice one' to everybody. Instead why not give ourselves permission to be nice to ourselves and respect our own energy, time, thoughts, opinions, wants and needs?

Many of us have a deep fear of abandonment so we go to any lengths to not upset other people as we fear they will walk away and we'll be left alone. We can run ourselves ragged worrying about whether we are good enough for him or her, and I did that for years. Now I honestly cannot care less what someone thinks of me, and it's an amazing and powerful feeling.

People can often be masters of words and throw words about that hit our hot-spots in order to sneakily force us to do what's good for them; beware of this and see it for what it is. We need to learn to stay calm, centred and in our own power by not reacting, and practise not reacting by staying true to ourselves. We can decide for ourselves what behaviours from others are unacceptable and inappropriate. We do not have to judge them or try and change them; we have to learn how to respond in a positive and healthy way.

It's so crucial to be directive about the parameters of our relationships. Relationships equal two people, so that means equal rights. We need to be able to define the relationship, and so does the other person. Once we express what our intentions are, we can't then take responsibility for how the other person reacts. Being honest and direct is the only policy, and why would we *not* want to be that way? We have every right to our needs, wants and bottom lines, and they have every right to their own. We have a right to make our own definitions and to ask questions and so do they. What we want is OK, and we need to accept that if someone else doesn't want what we want we can't stomp, sulk or manipulate them in order to make them feel guilty or shameful. That's passive controlling and it really does not work. We are not responsible for others feeling happy or feeling upset; we do not have that power and it is very arrogant to imagine that we are responsible. We also do not have to allow them any kind of power over us. We are completely free to choose our own feelings, thoughts and beliefs. I am aware that I keep repeating this, but it's important to do so.

Many of us freeze our feelings, deny our feelings, and fall for others telling us we are being selfish and putting ourselves first. However, we do not need to believe them. We can stop explaining, justifying and defending ourselves; we do not need to do this. We must give ourselves what we want and need, because we want and need it.

Denial is a powerful force, so never underestimate it. Doormats: find the courage to face things and not be victimised by life. Speak up, shine, strut your stuff, motivate yourself. Yes, you are more than capable of taking care of yourselves and you can start today by refusing to allow others to manipulate, guilt-trip and shame you into doing what is best for them. Ease up on pleasing everyone. Remember self-care is not selfish; it's self-esteem.

Divas: it is not your job to control people, outcomes, circumstances and opinions. You may not yet know this, but I am here to tell you that you are not God, and that no one has appointed you master of the universe. Back off with the self-righteous, loud and self-seeking arrogance. You need to look at deflating that ego, and replacing it with humility and grace. No one likes a big mouthed know-it-all, and no, it isn't being confident, it's being egotistical; they are two completely different things. You are not judge and jury, so where on earth do you get off on thinking you are?

I am only too well aware that change is difficult and scary and at times stressful, but to maximise our potential we need to make changes. We can either resist the changes or enjoy them; it's up to us. Change is brought about by attention and intention, and we always get what we seek.

Any thoughts of hatred, revenge and jealousy towards others are toxic. We have the power to change our thoughts from revenge to acceptance. Automatic thoughts are generated from old beliefs, so turning old, negative, toxic and destructive thoughts into positive, healthy and loving thoughts takes time, awareness and vigilance. Sometimes we need to give ourselves permission to change even though the people around us we love are not ready to make changes. We do not have to wait for them to gain awareness and a desire to change; we can move forward anyway. After all, if we waited we could be waiting forever, and why would we want to put our happiness on hold? That's crazy, right?

We do not need to stay with others who are happy waddling around in their dysfunctional behaviour, as they are accountable for themselves and we are accountable for ourselves.

So be good to yourself and start making changes – one step at a time, one day at a time!

Annie x

Reviews, reminders and resources

Annie's top reminders for Divas

- You can't change anyone else except yourself and the more you try to change someone else, the more they will resist.
- There is a difference between a demand and a request.
- Sulking, complaining, huffing, shouting and being controlling are *so* last season.
- It is neither your right nor your responsibility to flag up everyone else's shortcomings.
- Being hooked on yourself is an addiction.
- You need to resign as master of the universe.
- You are not God.
- Being critical, judgmental and defiant is not a good look.
- You must always ask before enforcing your unsolicited advice.
- Quit punishing others who do not act as you want them to.
- Lecturing other people pushes them away.
- God save us all from helpful people!
- Be clear on what you can change and what you can't.
- Quit focusing on the absence of perfection in others.
- Let go of any unrealistic expectations of others.
- Stop being so self-centred and give some thought to other people.
- Stop making other people's decisions for them.
- When you are aggressive, you will attract aggressive or passive-

aggressive people to you.
- Remember, nobody gets a kick out of being criticised.
- If you keep on being the rescuer, you will keep attracting needy people who want to be rescued.
- Stop lying to yourself about who you are. Be you!
- You may well have some good advice, but unless it's asked for, it isn't welcome or of any use to the recipient.
- You must not get so resentful when someone says no to you; get over it.
- When your partner is upset, offer them a hug, not an hour of analysis or advice.
- By all means have an opinion, but allow your partner to believe what they want.
- Give up the need to get the last word in.
- Remember, the lower your confidence and self-esteem, the greater your need to be right.
- Your reactions to your partner reflect your own shadow parts.
- Observe others' behaviour and feelings without judgment.
- Don't confuse vulnerability with weakness. People who have inner strength show their vulnerability.
- Check in with yourself: do you need to be needed?
- Telling people what to do is emotionally dominating them.
- Your opinion is just that – an opinion, not a fact.
- True giving is free; if you are keeping score, it's not giving.
- Start using your perceptiveness to build others up instead of putting them down.
- Keep your battered pride in a safe place until you have time to pause and re-evaluate, rather than lash out with your tongue.
- Stop punishing Doormats by sulking or withdrawing love, sex or money if they don't do what you want them to.
- Grow up; only children stomp and have hissy fits when they don't get what they want.
- Remember you are advertising your lack of confidence by being dominating and manipulative; confident people don't behave that way.
- Don't get so resentful when you are not being heard – only people without inner confidence need to be heard.

• Do you want to be right or do you want to be empowered?

• Successful people don't have the time to get hooked into other people's

business and lecture them; they have a life of their own.

Annie's top reminders for Doormats

• Stop putting everyone else on a pedestal and park yourself on one.

• One of the best things you can do is respect yourself enough to learn to listen and trust that inner voice.

• Give up being dependent on others for your identity.

• Stop being addicted to 'hope'.

• Let go of the fear of rejection.

• Assertively and politely hand Divas back the issues which they try to lay on you.

• Watch out for Divas' hooks, the methods they will use to get you to do what they want.

• Insist people ask directly for what they want from you rather than try to manipulate or shame you.

• Stop regarding yourself as being a notch or two lower than everyone else.

• Taking action will greatly rebuild your confidence.

• 'No' can be a complete sentence, and saying it does get easier with practise.

• Face your fears and take a chance on a new way of life.

• People-pleasing robs you of your power.

• You need to set and maintain your boundaries.

• Let go of the addiction to approval.

• State your needs and wants.

• You must value yourself.

• It's essential to build a relationship with yourself and get acquainted with who you are.

• Stand up and be heard, using the voice of reason and sanity.

- Stop denying your needs and being a martyr.
- Give up feeling defeated and take action.
- Learn to accept yourself exactly as you are.
- Stay aware of your behaviour, so you can transform it.
- Remember that self-esteem is not about who people are or what they have achieved; it's about how they feel about who they are and what they have achieved.
- Stop allowing others to walk all over you; be assertive.
- Say what you mean and mean what you say.
- Take the initiative if you're going out with a Diva.
- Stop tap-dancing around other people for affirmations.
- Give up the 'what ifs'; make a decision on what's acceptable to you, and stick with it.
- You are not responsible for how everyone else feels.
- Having a boundary will demonstrate to others how much you honour yourself.
- Find your voice and enjoy using it.
- Remember other people are not mind readers; they don't know what you want unless you tell them.
- Take responsibility for your words, actions and behaviours.
- Do not be pressurised by anyone; you can give yourself a day, a week, however long you need to decide what's right for you.
- Remember how amazing you are, even when someone else has treated you unfairly.
- Don't allow anyone to talk/shout at you; you can walk away.
- When saying no, you can look your partner in the eye and be firm, though also assertive.
- Do not destroy your self-worth by running your life on the basis of what others think of you.
- Be open to feedback, but do not plug into others' views for approval.
- Stop bingeing on self-pity.
- Don't follow the whims and dictates of everyone else's opinions.
- Stop allowing your emotions to bully you; instead start dancing with them.
- If you continue to give more than you get, only give to givers, stop giving to takers.

Weekly checklist

☐ This week, did you say no to someone who has been badgering you to do something you don't want to do?

☐ Were you honest this week about how you felt when asked?

☐ What insights did you gain this week?

☐ What changes have you made this week?

☐ What areas of your life do you feel need improvement?

☐ Did you ask for what you needed and wanted this week?

☐ Did you set any boundaries that needed to be set?

☐ Did you make excuses for any sabotaging behaviour?

☐ Did you defend or justify yourself to anyone?

☐ Did you bend yourself around someone to gain their approval?

☐ Did you say yes to someone when in fact you meant no?

☐ What are you most proud of this last week?

☐ Were you kind, compassionate and tolerant to others this week?

☐ Were your actions unkind, selfish and dishonest this week?

☐ Did you react to someone in an aggressive manner?

☐ When were you self-righteous, defiant and self-centred?

☐ Were you negative or positive this week?

☐ Did you take action?

☐ Did you feel any shame around anything?

☐ Did you allow anyone to talk at you?

☐ Did you use any assertive techniques?

☐ Did you get caught up in other people's dramas?

☐ Did you compromise your needs to keep someone happy?

☐ Were you trying to impress others rather than allowing them to impress you?

☐ What do you need to start doing, stop doing and continue doing?

Resourceful websites

SLA
www.slaauk.com
12-Step programme for sex and love addiction.

Coda
www.coda-uk.org
12-Step programme for co-dependency.

2-in-2-1
www.2-in-2-1.co.uk
Information on various aspects of relationship breakdowns.

Armchair Advice
www.armchairadvice.co.uk/relationships
Resources on practical relationship issues.

It's finished
www.itsfinished.com
Help, information and advice on relationship breakdown.

Anger management
www.angermanage.co.uk
Offering programmes and tools for controlling your anger.

AVP Britain
www.avpbritain.org.uk
Help for anyone being bullied.

Support Line
www.supportive.org.uk
Providing various information on emotional support groups
and counsellors.

British Association for Sexual and Relationship Therapy
www.basrt.org.uk
Information about psychosexual counsellors.

Trauma Clinic
www.traumaclinic.org.uk
Providing some practical support to victims of trauma.

Assist Trauma Care
www.assisttraumacare.org.uk
Offering some emotional support to victims of trauma.

Depression Alliance
www.depressionalliance.org
Offering various resources and tools.

Freedom Programme
www.freedomprogramme.co.uk
Offering help to women who have experienced any form of abuse.

Rights of women
www.rightsofwomen.org.uk
Legal advice and resources for women's rights.

Relate
www.relate.org.uk
0300 100 1234
For counselling, sex therapy and support for couples and families.

The Self Confidence Centre
www.selfconfidencecentre.com
07739 388072 / 020 7385 4741
Providing intuitive coaching, clinical hypnotherapy, EFT,
ThetaHealing and training for individuals and companies.

Complementary medicine and therapies

'Over 50% of GP Practices offer some sort of CAM.'
(Prince of Wales Foundation for Integrated Medicine)

To find a qualified lifecoach nationwide, visit:
Find a lifecoach
www.findalifecoach.co.uk
or
Lifecoach directory
www.lifecoach-directory.org.uk

To find a qualified hypnotherapist in your area, visit:
British Institute of Hypnotherapy
www.britishinstituteofhypnotherapy-nlp.co.uk
T: 01702 524484

Complementary Medical Association
www.The-CMA.Org.UK
T: 0845 129 8434

The Association for Professional Hypnosis and Psychotherapy
www.aphp.net
T: 01702 347691

The Register for Evidence-Based Hypnotherapy and Psychotherapy
www.rebhp.org
T: 0800 5300 586

To contact Noam Sagi or find a community of therapists offering a
broad range of treatments visit:
www.kingyotherapy.com
T: 020 7706 1997

To find a list of EFT practitioners nationwide, visit:
www.eftuniverse.com

Selected reading

Behrendt, Greg and Liz Tuccillo; *He's Just Not That Into You*, Simon Spotlight Entertainment, New York.

Blanton, Brad; *Practising Radical Honesty*, Sparrowhawk Publishing.

Brown, Byron; *Soul without Shame: A Guide to Liberating Yourself from the Judge Within*, Shambhala Publishers.

Burns, David; *Ten Days To Self-Esteem*, William Morrow & Sons.

Butler, Pamela; *Talking To Yourself: Learning the Language of Self-Affirmation*, HarperCollins.

Canfield, Jack and Mark Victor Mansen; *Chicken Soup For Your Soul: Living your Dreams*, HCI Publishers.

Cloud, Dr Henry and Dr John Townsend; *Boundaries: When To Say Yes, When To Say No To Take Control Of Your Life*, Perseus.

Day, Laura; *Practical Intuition*, Broadway Books.

DeeRoo, Carleen and Carolyn DeRoo; *What's Right with Me: Positive Ways to Celebrate Your Strengths, Build Self-Esteem and Reach Your Potential*, New Harbinger Publications.

Dillon, Stephanie and Christina Benson; *The Women's Guide to Total Self-Esteem: The Eight Secrets You Need to Know*, New Harbinger Publications.

Dutton, Donald; *The Abusive Personality*, Guildford Press.

Elgin, Suzette; *You Can't say That To Me! Stopping the Pain of Verbal Abuse*, Wiley and Sons.

Evans, Patricia; *The Verbally Abusive Relationship*, Holbrook Publishers.

Gawain, Shakti; *Developing Intuition*, New World Library.

Hay, Louise; *You can Heal Your Life*, Hay House Publishers.

Helmstetter, Shad; *What to Say When You Talk to Yourself*, Pocket Books.

Hendricks, Gay and Kathlyn Hendricks; *New Conscious Loving; The Journey to Co-Commitment*, Bantam Books.

Jeffers, Susan; *Feel The Fear and Do It Anyway*, Ballantine Publishers.

Jordan, Paul and Margaret Jordan; *Do I have To Give Up Me to Be Loved By You*, Compcare Publishers.

Katherine, Anne; *Boundaries: Where You End And I Begin*, Fireside Publishers.

Marshall, Megan; *The Cost of Loving: Women and the New Fear of Intimacy*, G.P. Puttman Publishers.

McKay, Matthew and Patrick Fanning; *Self-esteem: A Proven Program of Cognitive Techniques for Assessing, Improving, and Maintaining Your Self-Esteem*, New Harbinger Publications.

Mitchell, W.; *It's Not What Happens To You, It's What You Do About It*, Phoenix Press.

Mornell, Pierre; *Passive Men, Wild Women*, Ballantine Publishers.

Murphy, Dr Joseph; *The Power of Your Subconscious Mind*, Bantam Books.

Norwood, Robin; *Women Who Love Too Much: When You Keep Wishing and Hoping He will Change*, Tarcher.

Robinson, Jane; *Women Out Of Bounds*, Carroll & Graff Publishers.

Robinson, Lynne A.; *Divine Intuition: Your guide to creating a life you love*, Dorling Kindersley.

Ruiz, Don Miguel; *The Four Agreements*, Don Allen Publishers.

Ruiz, Don Miguel; *The Fifth Agreement*, Don Allen Publishers.

Ruiz, Don Miguel; *The Mastery of Love: A Practical Guide to The Art of Relationships*, Don Allen Publishers.

Scutz, Will; *The Truth Option*, Ten Speed Press.

Smith, Manuel J.; *When I Say No I Feel Guilty*, Bantam Publishers

Tolle, Eckhart; *The Power of Now*, New World Library.

Index

The Self-Confidence Centre

Annie Ashdown is one of Britain's leading coaches and founder of The Self-Confidence Centre in Harley Street, London, W1. Annie specialises in intuitive coaching, emotional freedom technique, theta healing and is a master clinical hypnotherapist and licensed Louise Hay teacher.

Annie's engaging personality and real life experiences have made her popular with the media and she is a regular guest expert on television and radio as well as a frequent contributor to magazines.

It was after working through her own difficulties that Annie recognised the tangible benefits that coaching can bring to so many parts of our lives. Following a successful career in film and television between Los Angeles, New York and London, Annie hit rock bottom in her personal and professional lives. She overcame a severe eating disorder, sparking a journey of self discovery and profound change, and decided to switch career direction to help others gain confidence, raise self-esteem and maximise their potential. Annie was a judge in 2009 on Britain's Next Top Coach and has a diverse list of clients in both the UK and the USA, including a host of celebrities. She is passionate about supporting women, offering them practical tools to be assertive in a non-aggressive way. Annie's 'tough love' approach is practical and down-to-earth, but tempered with a dose of humour and more often than not related to her own life experiences.

Annie is also co-founder of www.WomenMpoweringWomen. com, an online global platform where some of the most inspirational, influential, powerful female leaders and celebrities from the world of fashion, sport, entertainment, business and politics share their insights, tips and experience to motivate other women.

Annie is fully insured and a member of the British Institute of Hypnotherapy, Association for Professional Hypnosis and Psychotherapists, NHS Directory, Register for Evidence Based Hypnotherapy and Psychotherapy, Association Of Meridian Energy Therapists, and Complimentary Medical Association.

To purchase and download Annie's hypnotic MP3s on building confidence, experiencing total relaxation, losing weight and sleeping deeply (among others), as well as 101 affirmations on how to become empowered, raise self-confidence and boost self-esteem visit www.selfconfidencecentre.com.

Annie Ashdown

Personal coaching

These 60 minute sessions with Annie include unlimited email in-between sessions and take place face to face in Harley Street, London, W1 or can be conducted by phone. Annie is a results-based coach and offers practical tools to make significant breakthroughs. Check out testimonials on www.selfconfidencecentre.com

Training and workshops

Annie is a highly sought after NLP trainer bringing energy, compassion and humour to her bespoke workshops for individuals – 'Empowering women', 'Cocktails and coaching', 'Courage, confidence and charisma' and 'Doormat nor Diva be'. For corporate companies and government agencies she offers 'Leadership skills', 'Personal impact skills', 'Assertiveness techniques', 'Train the trainer', 'Non verbal communication skills', 'Conflict management', 'Verbal communication skills' and 'Confidence building'.

Annie is also part of an exclusive team of leading trainers delivering one day TV media training and one day crisis management training for key personnel at corporate companies, government agencies, and charities delivered at the Associated Press's new TV studios in Central London.

Speaking engagements

Annie has been a motivational speaker for ten years and has been invited to talk by many companies, groups and organisations including the Mind Body Spirit Festival, the Everywoman Annual Conference, Waterstone's, Chelsea Football Club, Orange, Royal Borough of Kensington and Chelsea, Vertu, Nokia, ITV, Sky, American Express, the Department of Work and Pensions, Job Centre Plus, Business Link , Women in Film and TV and many more.

If you know anyone who could benefit from the information in this book, want to send someone a copy of this book, or let Annie know how Doormat nor Diva be has brought you awareness, insights and tools to help you make changes please drop her a line at annie@ selfconfidencecentre.com.

Web pages

The Self Confidence Centre
www.selfconfidencecentre.com

Women Mpowering Women
www.womenmpowcringwomen.com

Facebook
www.profile.to//SelfConfidenceCentre

Twitter
SCCentre

LinkedIn
http://www.linkedin.com/pub/annie-ashdown/1/507/742

YouTube
www.youtube.com/user/SelfConfidenceCentre

Journal notes